The Adventures of
Loki - The Husky

The Adventures of Loki - The Husky

A Child's Emotional Sojourn

Krishna Vemuri/Dev Gupta

To order additional copies of this book, contact:
Xlibris
844-714-8691
www.Xlibris.com
Orders@Xlibris.com
821160

CONTENTS

To my father Ramagopal Vemuri, my mother Visalakshmi
Vemuri, and my uncle Narasimarao Vemuri.
—Krishna Vemuri

To my mother and my wife for always believing.
—Dev Gupta

PREFACE

The longer we look into them, the deeper the ocean of possibilities seems to be. In their essence, a baby's eyes are God's ultimate totems of purity, the purity of love.

When the baby grows into a teen and then into an adult, something changes about those eyes. Somehow they seem to lose the purity of love. It's quite the opposite story when you look at a dog's eyes—they are pure when they are born, they are pure the day they die, and they are pure every day in between. They shower love on humans all through their lives.

However, dogs barely get a chance to show the same unconditional love to their own species because they live in a human-centric universe where humans call the shots. Someone once said humans need dogs because there is no other way for them to experience pure love.

Has anyone ever wondered how things would be if dogs got to call the shots? Would a dog mother ever let her baby go? Would a pup ever leave her mother's side? Highly unlikely, because in their capacity to love, a human mother is a bear mother, is a whale mother, is a squirrel mother, is a dog mother.

*   *   *

ACKNOWLEDGMENT

I hereby acknowledge the contribution of my kids, Sourya Vemuri and Spurti Vemuri, and my wife, Dr. Swapna Vemuri, who introduced me to the beautiful dog-verse.

I thank my coauthor, Dev Gupta, for believing the huge project and walking this journey with me for the last two years.

I thank my colleagues at work who encouraged me with the idea of this story.

Krishna Vemuri

*   *   *

I thank my teacher, Mr. Biswanath Palit, who saw a writer in me long before I did.

My sincere gratitude to Mr. Krishna Vemuri for giving me the opportunity to work with him on his dream project.

Dev Gupta

Chapter 1

F5: Origins

Pie in the Sky

The kind of shoes you wear decides how far you go in life.

The first memory of my mother is from the time I was six months old. In the interest of honest storytelling, I will not play suspense with you at the start—it was a dream! But my friend, Weekday, has had long-tail differences with lesser scholars on whether dreams with over 60 percent retention value should qualify as legit memories. There's a philosophical split on that, and it's a lengthy thesis. I will get back on that later (or sign you up for a webinar with Weekday). For now, Mom!

From what I saw in the dream, Mom looked the same color as me. Oh, I forgot. My name is Loki. I am a husky, I take care of a big human family, and I absolutely love it when it snows. Since you are already here,

I'll declare this upfront: I am sharing this story with you not because it's good and worth reading, but because Weekday says that we must *not* go after anything *good*. Life's too short for *good*. You focus on THE BEST only.

Mom's the same cute shade of gray like me. She was big enough for me to roll in and hide inside her furs without you even noticing. The big dog was all licking and loving us siblings when I first saw her. Of the siblings, there were quite a few—I think I saw five or six of those poor souls right away. I still remember how all of us smelled mildly alike and yet distinctly different from the other. I always remember how Mom and each of my siblings smelled to this day. Whenever I see a husky down the road, I try to get a closer nose in just to find out if they're from my clan.

My siblings! Again. The cool thing was they were all trying to fake my look and get famous overnight. I must confess it was extremely flattering. But hey! Deadpool did not become Deadpool by playing dead. That guy died a few times—for real. Now that is the level of commitment I expect from every bloke lucky enough to be in my general vicinity. Yes, Deadpool qualifies by default.

Deadpool qualifies by default, and you are eligible because I always start with trust when judging new people, also because you kind of scored an elite membership by paying to read my story. But I must warn you at this point—you cancel yourself out at the slightest drop of enthusiasm.

The impression I made of Mom was pretty and warm. Mind you, that's not the same as "warm and pretty." The order in which you arrange words in a definition tells me a lot about the general direction your personality is heading.

Attentive ears, gentle manners, and a peculiarly long and furry tail—I think I even caught a couple of pretenders using her tail as the centerline for some silly who-hops-first game— you know, all that cuddly dogs and puppies YouTube stuff and what-not!

"Mom, Mom. I feel my stomach needs some blessing of food." I looked at Mom intently.

"Wake up, Loki, you're gonna miss daycare," Mom said in a strange, grave voice— very strange and very grave, as grave as a grown-up human male.

"What happened to your voice, Mom?" I was immediately concerned.

"Wake up, Loki, we don't want to miss daycare." It was dad running his soft hand through the back of my neck. My world! Another dream about Mom brought to a screeching halt by the cruel hand of fate. It wasn't another one. It was the same dream over and over. For some odd reason, I couldn't make it beyond the first two scenes. Yes, I address my human parents as Mom and Dad.

Generally, every day, it would be me waking up everyone else in the house, but I feel peculiarly lazy today. My human parents, brother, and sister would often talk among themselves about how their mornings changed forever after I entered their lives. I take full credit for that. It fills my heart, to be honest. They couldn't thank me enough.

At daycare, we often talk about how we are lucky enough to have both dog and human parents. But it's just the super lucky ones that get to live with all dog parents and siblings. Weekday is the only guy among us close pals who lived with this dog and human family simultaneously.

Another recurring theme of our daycare discussions is "the purpose of dogs." Why do dogs even exist? Are we here just for the humans like so many of us and the entire dog-loving human race seem to believe? Weekday slams a load of that blame on Hollywood that wouldn't tell the story any differently!

Oh sorry! I veered again. So mornings. There's a verse in the long song that the Creator dedicated exclusively to us dogs. It categorically talks about the kind of relationship dogs share with humans. To be honest, I do not remember much of that verse. But I'll paraphrase for you the part that I do: "Make their mornings worth it."

I think I can speak for my community here when I say every single one of us lives by that doctrine. Come morning, and we'll show you a thousand reasons why life is beautiful. Now we try and transmit those through the tongue so you might want to upgrade your infrastructure if the signals haven't been reaching you. You just could be missing out on some vital info there.

I got going right the next morning after I came home. But darn! Those beds are tall for a dog that's yet to hit his growth spurt. Notwithstanding that, with the amazing blessing of casting a cute pout on our faces almost at will, dogs can make humans do wonders. That morning, and every other morning thereafter, I took upon my young shoulders the responsibility of getting the family started bright and happy.

My parents pamper and cuddle me like I am their child. They gave me my anthem, a separate diet, and the entire backyard for fun and games. You can't blame me for indulgence either. No child ever says no to his parents' gifts. Oh, how could I forget? I have two human siblings too. Both of them go to college and are only home during vacations/weekends. On odd days, they pamper the wits out of me and often call their friends home to show off their baby brother's tail!

The best part is the love and hugs that follow when my parents tell visitors that I am a sweet and obedient child. Again, "sweet and obedient" is not equal to "obedient and sweet."

This morning, I wasn't feeling particularly enthusiastic. "Are we going to daycare or not?" Dad meant business. In the next thirty minutes, we had our breakfast and got ready for daycare. I flung to my car seat before Dad and Mom clicked at least a dozen and a half pictures of me.

The twenty-minute car drive from home to daycare is my best time of the day. And that's partly because of my car. It's a BMW 428i hardtop convertible, almost as good-looking as me. We have a few cars, but you could say the BMW is my favorite. My dad keeps telling his friends it's my car. But for some strange reason, he never lets me drive it. Then you do what you have to— you watch, and you learn. Rest assured, I know of how every single bell and whistle in that moving machine. I am rolling around with that beauty sooner than later.

Daycare for dogs is like school for humans. Day one is purely unidirectional violence and largely irreversible too. You don't ask for it, nor you do a thing to incite it. But it happens anyway. It's like the society's way of introducing torture into the lives of organisms whose minds and bodies are too fragile to gestate any possibility of exacting revenge. I am sure the first day at school was the first time Deadpool died! No kidding!

But once you are inside schools and daycares, you realize one of the most significant truths of life. Your tragedy is not always movie material. In a few weeks, you realize daycare is not that much of a disaster beyond the first day. Not sure if I can say the same thing about school though. At any rate, much of your comfort inside those institutions depends on how soon you can make cool friends.

We built from scratch a gang of some wholehearted power rangers at a daycare stacked with some wholesomely pretentious pricks. The friends I made at the daycare were perhaps the best friends you could ask for. I am sure you will love them as much as I do!

Kiko is generally the first one I see at daycare. She keeps hanging out by the gate every day until I arrive but strictly maintains that she's just "checking out the weather." Today was no different.

"Yo, Kiko, how are you?" I called out to her. "Where are Weekday, Pixie, and Luke?" I added.

"Hi, Loks, me good. How are you, buddy? Those fellas aren't here yet," Kiko spurted while walking toward me.

"Great! We will wait for them here, like we do every day." I walked up to her, chin-wagging affectionately.

Kickass Kiko

Hey there! My name is Kiko, and I am an Akita. I am half American, half Japanese, and the reincarnation of the Akita that Helen Keller owned. To be honest, I don't know a thing about my origins. Nor do I know nor have I ever seen my dog parents. I genuinely believe that human companionship is the chief purpose of a dog's life.

It's just me and my dad, Alan, at home. He is the source of power, inspiration, and courage in my life. He is a wizard by profession, and it's his hobby to beat pro athletes on the race track. Wizardry is easily his real thing. We have an unsaid, hidden understanding to never talk about it to anyone, including ourselves. All that Dad and I focus on is my athletic training so that, in time, I can end up being something close to a wiz myself. I could show you some tricks too, but Weekday says what's secret must stay that way.

I look forward to meeting my friends at the daycare now and then. The F5 is the best thing that happened to me after I found Dad. Loki is the best in that lot. If you are wondering who the F5 is, it is our gang of power rangers Loki just told you about a while back. You know Loki and me already. You will shortly know the others too. I don't know if it was the F5 at the daycare or my love for diversity that brought me close to them in the first place.

My hobbies include running, running faster, and mostly running after Dad. While I treasure all kinds of love for adventure, I hate travel of the other kind—the annoying business type where the only fun part is to watch Dad do his thing and make some real pros look like cats in a wild goose chase.

Honestly, I don't get along with folks all that easily. But to the few friends I have, I am loyal like a dog. While the F5 and other daycare mates do not particularly acknowledge my wisdom in magic and sorcery, I never really shy away from sharing my insights on things under my sphere. Besides sorcery, running, and Helen Keller, you could speak to me about smartphone apps, carb-free desserts, wireless device charging, and of course, Deadpool.

So that you know, I am the only dog in the F5 that can challenge Loki for a run. Challenge me in snow, and even the quick Loki is no match for my speed.

I do not remember where I was born. But I do know that before Dad, I used to live with Andrew and Nikita. They seemed like a happy couple until the day Nikita packed her bags, left, and never came back. Andrew would still care for me and would get me whatever I needed. But he was never the same person after Nikita left. After days of self-imposed silence, he took to drinking. Slowly, it started telling on him.

Before my very eyes, I saw Andrew sink deeper and deeper into a hole of his digging. He would barely speak to anyone unless it became necessary. I still found his heart to be kind and loving toward me, but I could also sense the hollowness overpowering him. I would gaze at him for hours at a stretch, hoping that he would finally say something or maybe even take me out for a walk. That never happened. A certain strange kind of bleakness engulfed the entire house. I started feeling weak.

Nikita never came back. I had begun missing her and the happy Andrew. For the little time that I had known Andrew, he was not a very social person. Nikita and I were the only family he had. I don't understand why Nikita left us. She was there one night, and the next morning she wasn't.

Where did she go? I would often think to myself. *Why on earth was she not coming back? Did she even care about me? Us?*

Thoughts like these kept floating on a sea of bleakness in my head. Until one day, when everything turned upside down, Andrew had been speaking over the phone for over twenty minutes. He was calm at first. Then the conversation turned ugly, so ugly that he started yelling, yelling like a man who had just lost his job.

That night Andrew did not let me enter the house. He shut the door and vanished inside. At first, I did not understand what was happening. I didn't know if he realized he'd shut the door on me. What I did know was he was in pain. I wanted to stay close to him. I did not want him to feel lonely. I barked loudly to let him know I was outside. He did not listen. No one listened. I realized he had done it on purpose. Andrew did not want to see me anywhere near him. That was way colder than his usual self. Maybe that was his way of saying, "Jump across the fence and never be seen around the neighborhood."

The next morning Andrew acted as if I did not exist. He did not take me out for our usual walk. He just brought my food bowl out and left some food in it—no call, no love, no pampering, only breakfast. My heart sank. He always took me out for a walk before breakfast. I never had my breakfast outside the house. The pampered child in me cried rebellion.

Right there, I did not like the way Andrew treated me—he had never treated me so harshly before. While he was going back, I looked at him and said a soft bark. He looked away and started walking back into the house. I barked again, this time louder. Andrew turned back and looked at me with pity. Then as if some deranged evil had taken over him, he went back inside and slammed the door behind him.

That slam of the door pounded straight into my heart as if it hurt me physically. I felt the impact like a sharp pang on my ribs. My immediate reaction was aghast with shock and pain— shock more than pain.

That thud in the chest was the first of many. Andrew started ignoring my existence altogether. I do not mean to exaggerate, but for a dog, not receiving enough love is tantamount to a hundred lashes every day. My soul was hurting with pain and anguish. I wasn't allowed inside the home anymore, even when it rained. He'd also stopped bathing me. All I managed was soft whimpers and hoped that Andrew would at least let me in the house when it rained.

In my heart, I would console myself thinking things would fall back to normal once Andrew get his job back. Like Nikita, the job never came back. Old Andrew had gotten sick, and after a point, his only interaction with the living world was to vent his anger on me. He even beat me physically a couple of times. I had to bear it all. Do dogs always have to endure things because their masters are having off time? Maybe I just had no other option. Also, because every dog I had met in my life always said we owed nothing but love and respect to our human parents.

It went on for three weeks. My body was on the verge of giving up. You could ask why I didn't just leave. Honestly, I still do not know why. Maybe I had a deep, self-harming sense of empathy for my human. Perhaps I had given up on the hope of life, just like Andrew. Or maybe, just maybe, my hanging around Andrew might have given him some speck of a reason to hang on to his own life.

Then one day, like an angel from heaven, Dad saw me and the pain in my eyes and the disgust in Andrew's while he was laying a wreath on his sanity. Dad shot a video of Andrew leaving me out on a rainy night. He called the police and showed it to them. Andrew pleaded guilty before the police and told them that I couldn't stay with him because he had no money. He couldn't let me off either because he said he loved me. He said he missed his wife Nikita and that I'd continuously remind him of her.

The police questioned Andrew on beating me. At first, he wouldn't give a thing, except for the tears that rolled out of his eyes. He would beat me in the hope that I would break the gate and just run away. Andrew told the police that he'd beat himself up every time he'd hit me. He showed them several marks of self-inflicted bruises on his own body.

I couldn't decide which possibility was more depressing, that Andrew would keep sinking deeper into that hole or that I would no longer be there by his side when that happens. Even if I wanted to stay, there was no way the police would let Andrew keep me. Besides, I wanted the meaningless suffering to end for both of us.

That was that with Andrew. I left him with no hard feelings in my heart and hoped he'd fight whatever demon was hiding in him.

The police took me in and let me by myself and started an active search for foster parents. When Dad came to know that they were looking for a permanent home for me, he at once decided to adopt me. I walked into the house of Alan Silverman, right next to the door of Andrew. It took somewhere between twelve hours and a day for Alan and myself to become dad and child. That was two years back.

Before I came to Dad's home, I would only hear stories about a national black athlete living in the neighborhood. It was after I moved into his house that I came to know that he was a real living wiz. The charm and affluence, the kindness, the love he showers on me—sometimes I wonder if I receive more than I deserve. Dad is such a kind person, and he even let Andrew come to his home and meet with me after he'd apologized.

Dad is single, sports being his only dedication. He had more national event golds than the rest of our town combined. He often travels to far corners of the country for competitions. I go out with him every time. It's such a joy to see Dad hit the gas on the race track and win it for me every time. It's even more fun when I join him in his training, and we race each other.

Some of Dad's latest trips have been more business-oriented, with him wearing suits and clunky ties. Such travels are boring to the hilt. Dad is Dad, and he never gets me wrong. When he realized I was getting bored with the business tours, he would drop me at the daycare. The father's wise decision opened up the gates of another realm of fun for me.

I realized it was so much fun to stay with other dogs at daycare. There were Loki, Weekday, Pixie, Luke, and dozens of other dogs who together made it all so starry during the day! When not with Dad or my daycare mates to bother me, I take out time to sympathize with cats that wanted to be born as dogs.

Today I got up early. Dad was still sleeping when I woke up. I love it when I wake up before Dad to catch that look of sheer pleasantness on his face. While I tried hard to let him sleep, you can't blame a dog for siding with her instincts. I climbed up Dad's bed and rubbed my moist nose against his cheek. He saw me and stretched out his arms for me. I did a short leap of faith and fit right in. The niceness and coziness of that feeling—ah, I cannot tell you!

It's one thing to hug someone, and it's something else to get embraced in return, especially when it is Dad. "Wait on, Kiko, we will go out for a jog," Dad said in his magical voice. We headed out for our usual morning jog at the park. At the park, we met with other dogs Jenni, Toby, and Bharav and greeted one another. You could say some lopsided dog pampering followed.

An exciting feature of our park jogs is my growing interaction with other humans in the park. I quickly learned Dad wasn't the only loving person around. It's incredible how everyone who sees me involuntarily wears their best smile of the day. I have to wag my tail tirelessly the entire time at the park. This bond that we share is one of the many reasons I tell everyone that humans and dogs are meant to be. Dogs are for humans after all!

We followed up the jog in the park with a quick shoreline sprinting dash and came back home. Dad made me a delicious meal. He's heading out on another business trip later today. That means it's another day at the daycare!

I'd tell you, daycare kicks the boring out of life for single dogs with single parents. I've never been within miles of boredom when Dad is home. But once Dad is gone, it feels like the whole house—every brick, door, and curtain—is coming to bite you in the butt. Thanks to daycare, the brick, door, and curtain were replaced by Weekday, Loki, and Luke. And since it was Friday, I got a bonus— Pixie too!

As friends, the five of us stick together through thick and thin and then some more. I think I am ready for another day of F5. Just like the odd other day, it looks like I am the first one at the daycare waiting for the others. There, Loki is second in the race, as always.

"Yo, Kiko, how are you?" Loki called out from a distance. "Where are Weekday, Pixie and Luke?" he added.

"Hi, Loks, me good. How are you, buddy? Those fellas aren't here yet," I spurted while walking toward him.

"Great! We will wait for them here like we do every day." Loki walked down toward me, chin-wagging at how bright the day was.

"Is that a breathing haystack walking toward us, or has Mother Nature blessed us with another day of Weekday?" I took the first shot at Weekday even as he was making his way to the ring.

"I am a haystack any old day of the week." Weekday had heard it. And like every time, he was ready to give it back.

You have friends, and then you have uncles from past lives disguised as friends. Meet Weekday.

When Weekday talks, the rest of us listen. When he walks, the rest of us laugh. Not that he has a limp of something (that'd be rude), but it's the other thing he does with his body hair, which we think is super funny. But boy, he knows stuff! He claims to have a repository of 8,000 smells, of which I have personally verified at least 3,286. Now Weekday is as sharp as they get— give him a situation, and he will have advice served to you on a gold plate. Speak of smartness and the only person who belongs to Weekday's league is Deadpool, as famously noted by Loki. Now Loki comes across as a true fan and no pretentious wannabe.

"Okay, haystack! How are you?" I poked back at Weekday's nose.

"Good, and how are you? And you, Loki boy, wassup?" Weekday greeted back with a grin!

"All sun and stars. How are you this morning?" Loki answered.

"Good, like I said." Weekday looked at the road leading up to the daycare like he was trying to spot someone else.

"Where's Luke and Pixie?" Loki asked.

"No sight of them yet." Weekday looked out some more.

A Day of Weekday

There's a reason or two the F5 listens to me! I flaunt what I got, and I got quite a lot. Some speculate that had it not been for the daycare classes I give, I could have ended up a professor of dog studies at Yale or Princeton or maybe even at MIT. But in all honesty, I am only as regular as any other dog, with some additional puddings here and there.

Right then. My name is Weekday, and I am a bearded collie, aged five. The earliest memory of my existence goes back to the time I was living with five of my siblings in the family of an elderly couple, Henry and Sylvia, both of them local university professors, loved and respected by the community. Hen and Syl have been the gentlest people even on their worst days, from what I have known of them. They have three children, all reasonably well-off and living in nearby towns.

By scholarly estimates, I was one of the most fortunate dogs in the country. That's because not many bred-for-sale dogs get to stay with their dog families. I did. Mine was the most innocently loud childhood you could imagine for a dog. I lived with my mom Beth and siblings Cherry, Ginger, John, and Superdog. Yeah, big family for a pet dog, more so because the smart one (that would be me) got to steer the others around the house. Nevertheless, ours was a big happy family of six dogs and two humans.

Now my life with mom and my siblings was bizarrely similar to one of Loki's recurring dreams, where he keeps seeing his mom and siblings doing cozy and having fun together. When Loki first told me about those dreams, I could not believe my ears. My siblings and I have pulled off every stupid stuff that Loki dreams about many times. Yes, there was the mindless tail-hopping too!

Loki and I often talk about whether all this was just a coincidence or there could be something more to it. While Luke and Pixie seem to err on the side of the accident, Kiko, Loki, and I always feel there's some kind of strange signaling hidden in those dreams. Maybe we were about to find out soon!

If anything, my childhood was the amplified version of Loki's dreams. I remember every bit of it like it happened yesterday. The cuddles and love from Mom, the protection and shelter from Henry and Sylvia, the timely ice cream and cheesecakes, the play at the park with all other neighborhood dogs—it was a fairytale if I must be honest. Speaking of Henry and Sylvia, they were sailing over the moon. There was nothing they wouldn't have done for us in a heartbeat.

A few incidents are incredibly dear to me, in addition to the regular play and puppy love. This particular incident I am about to tell you is from the time Mom was the happy mother of five five-day-old puppies. Mom's whelping fatigue was vaguely behind her, and she was all lovey-cuddling her litter.

That day Henry came up with this squarely genius idea of poking fun at Mom. He spread John, Cherry, Superdog, Ginger, and myself on an open carton tray. We barely had eyes back then. At first, Mom did not mind much. Either Henry or Sylvia would do it every day since our birth. They would clean us with moistened soft tissue and check if anyone of us opened our eyes or had any wounds. Mom kept wagging her tail as Henry began wiping us with a soft cloth.

Suddenly, Hen stepped up the game. He lifted the carton tray and carefully extended his arms over the head, holding the plate about six and a half feet above the ground. Mom sat up, mildly fuming, and confused at what Henry was trying to do. Henry looked at Mom. He slowly brought us down and placed the tray back on the floor. But the mischief wasn't over then. He put his hands over the tray an inch over us and did a little DJ thing with his hands for a few seconds, giving Mom the impression that he was rolling us over one another. Mom gushed and fizzed. She leaped and sat upright between Henry and us.

Henry continued with his air-DJ gig, never really touching or harming us in any manner though. Mom acted all funny and held off Henry's hands with her paws every time he brought them near us. He kept doing silly stuff with us to irk Mom. Mom, being Mom, kept shadow-boxing him all the while. I barely had my eyes pop on me, and it was still too much fun to ignore.

Now Mom knew it all too well in her heart that Henry would fight a planet and a half to keep us safe. That's how mothers are—all the mothers on earth. They get worked up at the slightest hint of trouble for their children. And you and I can't do a thing to change that.

Another day Henry brought a baby monkey from one of his university colleagues and sneaked him into the carton tray with us. For half a day, Mom didn't even realize there was a baby monkey in the tray. She kept licketty-loving us and the monkey. Just imagine a mini-monkey camouflaging as a dog pup. That stuff was hilarious to the hilt. The thing even drank milk from her, which made him our brother by accident.

Cherry, John, Ginger, Superdog, and I grew up like a tower of giraffes fighting for space. We made the house into a mad party of happiness. The elders in the house—Mom, Henry, and Sylvia—turned children with the children. They did have a hard time bringing us up. I can write it for you on recycled paper that they did a good rocking job at it. We kids would often talk among ourselves about how lucky we were to have a human and a dog family at the same time. Better still, they were the same family in the same place we call our home.

Stories like these would easily occupy half our conversations at daycare. Hear it from the horse's mouth—there's a strange kind of satisfaction in meeting and hearing out other nostalgic dogs. Loki, Kiko, Luke, and Pixie—everyone in the F5—all had some fantastic things to say. We would often kill time by hearing out one another's stories. With the stories, came memories, memories of lives lived differently.

Oh yes! The monkey kept coming back to our tray and later to our home as we grew up. It turned out, the monkey was rescued from traffickers after he'd lost his mother at the zoo. Henry's colleague from the university had adopted the monkey and moved into our neighborhood. Mom took the child under her wing and loved and raised him like her child. Sylvia lovingly named him Mama's Boy.

We made him a part of the gang just like that and got along together like wet butter on a hot pan. Besides all the extra fun, Mama's Boy ended up being a numerical advantage too. Since we'd snowballed from five to six, it became much more comfortable to divide teams for the games. That was his most significant role in our lives, and his multipurpose tail came a distant second. The daycare dogs still have a hard time believing we grew up with a monkey.

As we grew up, Mom, Henry, and Sylvia grew older. Henry and Sylvia's children, our human siblings, used to visit us every once in a while. They would care for us just as much as they would care for the elders. The best part was the gifts. Every time our human siblings visited us, they brought us presents—toys, funky food, clothes, swagger—all those things. Seasons passed; happiness didn't. Life was only getting brighter every day.

But what could be so permanent about a dog's life? Our sunshine days were numbered. Mom fell ill. The vet said it was perilous cancer tearing her entrails. The news fell on us like a hammer on a thin metal plate, shaking our very existence with disbelief. It took us a long time to come to terms with what we had just heard. Why Mom? Why us? Everything was going so well. We were having the time of our lives. Not anymore. A begrudging water cannon had blasted into our fireplace. It was shattering.

The day we came to know about Mom's illness, Henry called all the dogs in the neighborhood over to our house to see her. She was so gentle and caring and loved every dog in the community like they were her children. Mama's Boy would not leave her side even after everyone else had left. From that day until her last day, Mom's labored evenings found the company of loving animals.

Mom loved us deeply. During her last days, that love turned into all kinds of ugly. She would slide into paranoia every time one of us went off her sight. One of those days, she collapsed while caressing Superdog. The vet said it didn't look good for her. That fall had broken one of her legs. At her age and condition, she felt double the pain.

Our mother, the center of our universe, was in deep, irreversible pain. She was biting a long dry bullet. The cancer was killing her slowly. She became weak, so weak that we had to help her walk around the house on three legs. Henry quickly made arrangements for a prosthetic leg. That eased some of Mom's pain. However, she still needed help moving around. I would sit by her for hours together, cracking lame jokes, trying to get her to smile. The jokes were lame, but Mom did her best to muster a smile at each of them. A while later, I realized how difficult it was for her to smile, and I stopped with the jokes.

Despite all her pain and suffering, Mom was not willing to let us go. She was fighting illness at all levels—physical, emotional, and everything else. She knew she would not outlast her pain. But the old dog was still struggling with every bit and piece to stay with her children just that wee bit longer. Cherry, John, Ginger, Superdog, Mama's Boy, and I sat by her side day and night. As we were trying to comfort her, she kept drifting farther away from us one day at a time.

It was like Henry's game to irk Mom playing out all over again, only in its most ruthlessly demonic manner. Mom was fighting for her children, then she was fighting for her children all over again. Any lesser dog would have given up on life long ago. But my mom was no ordinary dog. She was the most amazingly fierce dog mother you could have ever seen.

The vets checked on Mom every second day. They had been doing it for weeks. At one point, I'd overheard them speaking to Henry. They spoke of something about an injection if Mom kept punching above her weight. What did that mean? I couldn't hold back. I told Mom about it. What followed was a conversation that shook me on the inside.

"Mom, can you hear me? We need to speak." I nudged her softly.

"Yes, my dear. Go on, tell me," Mom replied meekly.

"How did it go with the vet today?" I asked.

"As usual. The vet saw me, examined me at different places, said a couple of sweet words, shook her head, and left quietly," Mom said with an eerie stillness.

"I think I heard her speak to Henry," I said.

"Did you, dear? Tell me about it? How many more days do I have?" Mom tried her best to make herself sound funny. However, she only managed to look cocky.

"Mom, please. Never say that again. The doctor told Henry about some injection. She said you are punching above your weight. What's that supposed to mean, Mom?" My voice was choking up.

"That means your momma is not giving up easy, big boy." Mom's pain was searing.

"Please don't say that, Mom. Henry will do something. I am sure," I asserted.

"He has done it already, my dear." Mom suddenly sounded calm and continued, "He has done everything he could to keep me alive."

"He will fight a planet and a half to keep you happy. I know he will." Mom was breaking my heart with every word.

"Tell me that you will stay happy after I am gone. Promise me, Weekday." The old dog broke into a long sob.

I could not gather enough voice to answer Mom. I just cried like every child who's about to lose his mom, hoping against hope that a miracle would save her. That maybe, just maybe, Henry would pull off something one last time. But deep down, I knew we were seeing the last of her. The short-lived reality of existence stung my heart.

"Promise me that you will never leave Henry and Sylvia for the world," Mom came back.

I promised her that I would stay happy and do everything to keep Henry and Sylvia happy. Mom drifted into a lull of sleep.

I could not sleep that night. My heart was heavy. I went up to the terrace and sat there, gazing at the stars. On cloudless nights, there are thousands of stars in the sky. Will Mom become one of those stars as they showed in the movies? Is it true that all stars are lost parents who watch over their children and shed tears when they see we're unhappy? Will Mom also watch over us after she is gone? I'll never know.

The next morning the vet returned with two assistants. Sylvia, my siblings, and I gathered near Mom. Henry came into the room with the vets. He sank on his knees before Mom and started crying like a baby. It was time. The vet brought out an injection from her kit and asked Sylvia to hold Mom tight. Henry cried louder, his sobs distinctively longer. We cried with him. They gave her the injection. Mom was euthanized before my eyes! A strange sense of surrender spread across her as the light faded along with all her suffering. One dose and five dogs and a monkey became orphans.

The next few weeks were not easy. Nor for us. Nor for Henry and Sylvia. Time became the biggest riddle for me. Minutes became hours, hours swelled into days, days snowballed like weeks, weeks turned into months. I was continually brooding and brooding and brooding. Food wasn't tasty anymore, and the toys weren't inviting. People were uninteresting, and the siblings were unplayful. Existence became uneasy. Life itself had become a challenge. I realized how the loss of a parent meant the silent death of childhood for their children.

If it wasn't for the inexplicable care shown toward us by Sylvia and Henry, my siblings and I might never have recovered from what we had suffered. Henry was just as broken as I. He would barely speak to the rest of the neighborhood after Mom passed. She was his first pet, and he'd promised her he would never let her go. That was an unrealistic promise. Dogs do not outlive humans. Nevertheless, a promise was broken, and Henry blamed himself for it. He believed it was all his fault.

When everything seemed bleak, Sylvia rose to the occasion. The mother of three became the mother of nine, including Mama's Boy. She never let us out of her sight. When Henry was falling, she became his walking stick. When Superdog was grim, she humored him to a smile. When Cherry was depressed, she sang her a lullaby. When I was hopeless, she gave me hope. She told us it would pass like everything else. If kindness has a human form, that'd be Sylvia.

With Sylvia's help, Henry slowly recovered. He resumed taking us to the walks. He would take us to the park and let us play with other dogs in the neighborhood. Henry would sit by the bench and watch us play. At times he would stare blankly at us with no clue as to what was happening around him. On some days, Sylvia would join Henry by the bench on her way back from the store. Slowly, as time passed, the time at the park became our happiest hour of the day. Everything at home had Mom's memory etched on it. At the park, we slipped into oneness with the carefree universe.

For an hour in a day, we would forget what had happened and be lost in play. Hen and Syl would silently watch us play and smile from the bench. One of those days at the park, I wasn't feeling particularly well and skipped play. I sat beside Henry for a while as we watched my siblings and other dogs play. Sylvia joined us at the bench after a bit. We made small conversation, nothing much to note. I told them I wanted to take a walk around the periphery of the park and left the couple to talk to each other. My siblings did not mind my absence. John, Ginger, Cherry, and Superdog continued their play like every other day.

I saw dogs and people from all walks of life while walking around the park. Some seemed happy and content, while others were rather sad and gloomy. Those who were involved in the play were just playing, free from most emotions, just happy bundles of energy. Halfway through the circumference of the orbed park, I saw a deserted bench and a lonely Labrador crouching quietly near it. It was diametrically opposite to the bench where Henry and Sylvia were sitting. I looked around to see if the dog had a human companion. No one in the park seemed related to this dog. I went ahead and sat beside him.

"Hi," I said.

"Hey," he replied.

"I am Weekday. You seem to be alone here."

"Yes, I come here every day, this same spot. Haven't you seen me before? Name is Noah, by the way."

"Nice meeting you, Noah. We kind of keep to the other side of the park and the ground in the middle. Those four collies right there in the middle are my siblings. The old couple on the opposite end you see there, those are our humans." I tried being as soft and pleasant to the Lab as possible.

"And there you go, the monkey that just joined the couple, he is Mama's Boy, our brother by accident." Yes, Mama's Boy would often join our wagon to the park. He was kind of the center of attraction too, the lone monkey in a park full of humans and dogs. The monkey had grown up faster than any of us could have imagined.

"You got a big family," Noah said with compassionate affection.

"Yes, it was bigger when Mom was around." I sensed the pain in him.

"I am sorry." Noah tried to comfort me with similar wetness in his voice.

"It's okay, we are on our way to overcoming it." I tried to sound bright. "Where are your humans? And siblings?"

"I do not know if I have any siblings. My humans let me go." Noah tried to look at some distant point away from the park.

"That is so wrong. Why did your humans do that? Where do you live now?" I asked in surprise.

"I live in a nearby house. Don't get me wrong. I don't blame the boys for letting me go. I stayed with them for three years. They were a fraternity at the college in the next town, and I was their house dog. You know the innocent type they show in all those college movies. They poured all kinds of stuff on me, including love and care. But time ran out on them," Noah said with a sense of strange dispassion.

"College got over. No one was willing to take me to their homes. They said I belonged there, inside the campus. I thought I had a chance with the new lads that came in. But they got their puppy. That's how the script goes in those college flicks, no exceptions," Noah continued hurriedly.

"Sad to hear that. Did you come to our town after that? Did you find another home?" I was so full of questions for Noah.

"I thought I would hang around the college and stick to the memories we had there. But the boys thought I would not be safe there without them. They sent me up at this woman's house in this town through some adoption agency. That's my time. I should get going now. The old lady gets worried if I do not return on time. Good talk, buddy!" Noah rushed toward the horizon.

"Good talk, Noah." He was gone before I could say a proper goodbye.

I sat right at the spot Noah was seated, looking in the direction of Henry and Sylvia. They seemed content. Not particularly happy, but content. They kept looking at the dogs playing in the park like a child gazing at the stars. It had been over six weeks since Mom left us. Despite having one another, we were all like Noah in our strange little ways, feeling sore and unwanted. That's the thing about loneliness—it could strike you right in the middle of a crowd without the person next to you even knowing about it.

None of us had recovered in the real sense of the term. Our frequency of park visits would barely exceed one per month when Mom was still with us. The backyard used to be our park back then. Most of our neighborhood dogs would come over to play. Those were our days of unmatched glory. Neither my siblings nor I realized that the day Henry decided to take us to park after Mom was gone was the first time we looked outside of our house for happiness.

Our glory days were behind us, just like Noah's were behind him. But were our grief and pain bigger than Noah's? Or unlike him, were we just not ready to acknowledge our loneliness? We might never know. What I did know was we still had a family that we were sticking together through a rough time. What family did Noah have? Does he even know his siblings or have any? What if someone from his family was right there in this park? He just might have buried a bulk of his pain in that obscurity.

As I kept looking at Hen and Syl, the thoughts started fading away one by one. The old couple meant so much to each other. Their bond was such that they barely needed to speak to communicate. They would sit idly at the bench, hold hands, and look at the dogs playing in the park. That was their love—holding hands and looking outward in the same direction. What a wonderful feeling that must be, to be in love with someone without the vulnerability relationships bring, with someone who doesn't need to search for love in your eyes. I realized most couples who've bested the test of time over seasons are like that. There's a certitude in their bond that's miles beyond the temptations of youth.

That evening John and Cherry and Superdog and Ginger played as if they cared about nothing in the world. They looked all kinds of funny with some of their antics. I could not help laughing at myself at the thought of how stupid I must have looked while playing. That's how dogs are—pure and somewhat stupid animals always on the lookout for sport and love. It was funny how Superdog would leave all games in the middle and try and bite his tail. It's one of those rare things in dog movies that resembles some truth.

I sat steadfast near the bench, thinking all kinds of crazy things. I realized it was over an hour that we'd been in the park, and we were still playing. Generally, we'd keep playing until Henry beckoned us at the close of the hour. That evening Henry seemed to have lost time on us. He just held Sylvia's hand and kept looking. The dogs did dogs, and they kept playing.

I wanted to go home. Too many thoughts had tired me down. I slowly walked across the other half of the park and reached Henry and Sylvia. They were still brooding together, their gaze fixed at some distant void in the sky. The sun was just setting. A couple of stars were peeping down lazily from the sky. Their collective aura was such that time had frozen upon them. I quietly sat down nearby and let them be.

That evening we left the park after everyone else. The old couple broke out of their wafty slumber only after my siblings made some noise. We quietly drove our way back home.

I was barely hitting my adolescence around then. When you are in that phase of life, things like relationships are not easily understood. Yet the simplicity and innocent devotion between Henry and Sylvia, their sense of gratitude for having each other, their oft-used nonverbal communicative gestures—all that shaped my basic understanding of romantic relationships between adults. They were like a pair of twin stars that unconditionally revolve around each other.

That night I went to bed a little disappointed, in part because I could not play with my siblings and in part because of all the tiring thoughts from the day. I thought I would make up for it by playing some extra time the next day. Like all dogs devoid of play, I took refuge in the thought of the play.

Come the next day, I was all raring to go to the field and play. Henry accompanied us to the playground as usual. Sylvia was a little under the weather, so she decided to skip the store, park, and stayed back at home. Superdog and Mama's Boy stayed back at home with her.

Something exciting filled our eyes and imaginations when our eyes saw the first set of visuals from the park. A friendly dog rescue group had come with all types of outdoor sports equipment for dogs. They had small trampolines, inflatable toys, little foam objects serving no particular purpose, a couple of tall bells for the "jumping" types of ringing, and a lot of other playful stuff.

I am sure we ran into the ground faster than the speed of sound. "Careful!" Henry shouted from the bench as we lost ourselves in play. There was no way we were leaving the ground in an hour. To add to the fun, the dog rescue party had brought with them all the rescued dogs from their shelter!

New friends and new games, we were unwrapping a treat of an evening. An hour passed before we could even try all the games. The ground had become a freak show full of jumping dogs barking their lungs out in happiness. I could sense Henry was a little restless on the bench. The hour was over, and Henry was signaling us to come back. But what did Henry know about being a dog? We were having the time of our lives.

Unlucky Superdog and Mama's Boy! They were missing out on all the fun. Henry knew we were not leaving anytime soon and sat again on the bench. Thankfully, there were others like him to keep him company. One moment I saw Henry alone on the bench, and the other moment Superdog was there with him. Ah, news of that grand play must have reached little brother! He better joined us real soon. The fun was too much even to attempt to describe.

"Duck, Weekday!" Cherry shouted as someone threw a ball my way.

"My ball!" I yelled with joy and gave it a flying head butt with all my furry glory. I felt like liberation personified.

Wait, where did Superdog go? Wasn't he there a moment before? And Henry was missing too. They must have left in a hurry. Together. That was weird. Something didn't feel right. I looked at Cherry, John, and Ginger, and they were all devoured by play. I somehow managed to drag Cherry out of the noise and asked her, "Did you just see Superdog and Henry at the bench?"

"No, it's just Henry at the bench. Superdog didn't come to play today, remember?" Cherry signaled at the bench.

"Oh my god! Where is Henry?" Cherry yelled in shock, her contours shaping drastically. Henry never left the bench ever while we played.

"That's the thing." I tried to find my balance. "I saw Superdog running to Henry, and the next moment I looked, they weren't there, both of them." I ran up to check if Henry's car was still there. It wasn't.

"We gotta run." Cherry pulled John and Ginger out of the ground, and we steamed toward home. We all knew Sylvia was under the weather since morning. And the way things had been playing out, we naturally feared the worst. We'd generally take between fifteen and twenty minutes to stroll from our home to the park. But that was walking. We had covered half our way toward home in the next three minutes.

"Speed up!" I yelled. There was no sign of Henry's car at the store. That meant they left for home straight away. My heart was beating against my chest like an angry machine gun. I looked back at my siblings and signaled them to run faster.

Cherry could not run anymore. All drained from the play at the ground, she took to a panting stroll. "John, Ginger!" I shouted. "Stay with Cherry. Bring her home safe." I ran and kept running like a child chasing a falling kite. I kept picking pace because I knew in my heart what was to come. The kite was floating down like a waning arrow, and the child was too far. The sun was setting on Sylvia. I barely had the time to make it in. I had promised Mom I would keep Henry and Sylvia happy and never be far from their side.

Later that evening, another promise was broken. Humans and dogs assembled again to mourn another death. Sylvia, the closest link we had to a mother, had left us forever. The worst part is I will never know if she'd seen me for that last time. I remember that evening like it happened yesterday. It was like sliding into a trance when I ran into the house.

I could still smell life in Sylvia the moment as I was entering the house. Yet there was the faint smell of death too. There was another peculiar smell, that of a battle between life and death. I had never felt anything like that in my life. The woman did not want to go. She wasn't giving up, not before she could see all her children and animals. As she laid still on her deathbed, Superdog sat below the bed, still like a stone, letting out only soft whimpers.

Henry sat by her side on the bed, holding her hands in his, steadfastly looking at her face. He was saying something to her about things falling back in place very shortly. Henry wasn't ready to live life without the company of his loving wife. Henry held Sylvia's hands as tightly as he could, almost trying to prevent her from falling over to the other side physically. I looked at his face, and he looked like a helpless man, wholly demolished by the powers of nature.

Henry and Sylvia had lived so much together that they must have forgotten what it was like living alone. At that moment, his wife was slipping into the abyss. Henry did not even want to remember how living alone felt. As Henry was clasping onto Sylvia's hands, a particular realization dawned upon him. She wasn't waking up from that slumber. Henry knew better. He had seen death in the past, in the past that wasn't so distant either.

Henry lifted his sunken head from Sylvia's bosom and recollected himself like the brave man he is. He assured her, "Rest. Try and take rest. I'll take care of our children, all of them. I'll keep well, and I'll look after your plants too."

Sylvia's labored breaths slowly paced down, and her muscles let go of the tension. She lifted her right hand briefly for a second. And that was that. Henry's wife and our godmother, Sylvia, had left behind a full pack of aggrieved souls.

Our human siblings arrived a little later. They clung to us in grief like siblings cling to one another. Who else could realize the kind of pain we were going through better than them? For a brief while, we didn't feel like dogs and humans anymore. We were all motherless children under one roof. It was then that I stumbled upon a profound truth—in grief and suffering, we are all equal. I wish no child ever feels such pain and helplessness in their lives.

It was life-shattering to lose Sylvia. I had been on the receiving end of her unrelenting love for a long, long while. I couldn't help brooding over how unfairly the sun set on her. After she had left, I would often sit on the terrace all by myself and gaze vacantly into the ancient void of the night sky. We are humans and dogs, whales and trees, zebras and cockroaches, grasses and ferrets, plankton and raccoons, and millions of other things on the earth. And yet we're all just chance manifestations of stardust. Damn, the realization of it!

Small minds realizing meteoric truths is the quickest road to depression. The passing of Mom and Sylvia turned me into a sad, depressed dog. My siblings weren't doing any better either. Our collective burden fell on the aging shoulders of Henry. Boy! Did the old man not throw the kitchen sink at it! Henry swiftly employed an assistant to help with us, bought some hundred different dog toys, and applied for an additional weekly leave at the university. To be fair, he did every small and big thing he could do to make us feel more comfortable. After all, we were the only family he had after his children left home for their own lives.

But only the heart knows what it's truly lost. It's not easy to breathe life into five depressed dogs, particularly when you are depressed yourself. The depression started to show in Henry and us. The more he would try to love us, the more he remembered how his wife loved us. It quickly slipped from being an emotionally cumbersome task to a total psychological nightmare for him.

The family had seen two deaths in six weeks. Henry and his children knew what was needed. They knew we required care. They understood we needed happiness around us to be happy again. Henry's children, along with one of their friends, adopted Cherry, John, Ginger, and Superdog. I clung on to Henry. I wanted to stay with him, and I told him about the promise I had made to Mom. I had promised Mom I'd always rest with the old pair. Henry was my chance to fulfill at least half of that promise.

That was also the time I learned an essential lesson about promises: Both dogs and humans make way too many promises. Keeping some of those promises requires you to exercise control over the forces of nature like life and death. I promised myself not to make another false promise in this lifetime.

A week after Sylvia's demise, our siblings separated too. John, Ginger, Cherry, and Superdog promised me and one another that they'd keep meeting often. From eight happy souls chirping around the house like a band's chorus, we suddenly became two. The little world around us had broken into a million fragments. Sylvia and Mom were no more. My brothers and sisters left. All Henry and I were left with was boredom after a couple of days of silence and remorse.

We had two options at that point: We could either drown in the boredom or we could watch TV. We went ahead with TV. Both Henry and I started gorging upon loads and loads of dog movies. We started a little blog where we would cowrite a dog movie review every week. At first, we got limited visibility and reach. Slowly, more and more people started reading our reviews and appreciated our perspective.

We enjoyed watching movies, talking, and writing about them. I noticed that almost every dog movie had one thing in common: There's one or more heroic dogs (or they turn heroic sometime during the film), and they love humans. I am sorry, they don't just love humans—they love humans to the point where humans feel that "for dogs, no purpose of life is greater than serving humans."

When I shared this with Henry, we both agreed with it and kind of walked over it many times.

"Isn't that how it's supposed to be in the movies?" he said.

"Umm," I replied.

Now make no mistake. Every good movie makes dogs look like genuine heroes ready to do the right (and often brave) thing at the right time. But that doesn't iron out a powerful undercurrent that spells out in very bold lettering: DOGS ARE FOR HUMANS. The purpose of a dog is for humans exclusively, both in their happiness and sorrow!

The more thought I gave to it, the more convinced I became of the belief. I started observing it around me. Honestly, with the rare privilege of having lived with both a human and a dog family, I knew better. For most of our friends and daycare, including our F5 gang, the thought of a dog family was not just unreal, and it was also pretty scary.

"The girls would have to divide all that love and attention between another sibling and me, eww!" That was a rather recent one from Pixie.

But not every dog is allergic to the thought of siblings and parents. Some are intrigued by the proposition. Some like my dear pal Loki who lives in his dreams about his family are more than just paper castles of his imagination. He remarked in one of our recent conversations, "Do dreams come true at all? What do they say about dreams in our dog movies?"

I feel pretty lucky about myself when I see other dog kids at daycare. I can at least meet my siblings now and then at parties and family gatherings. Even the F5 has come to some of these parties. And we can't say we haven't enjoyed ourselves. To be honest, the daycare has given me much solace after my family withered away. I am just as happy going to daycare and spending time with other dogs as I am lazing around the house and watching TV with Henry.

Over the last few weeks, my visits to the daycare have been a lot more frequent, thanks to Henry's lecture assignments around the world. I don't mind being a boarder at daycare either. It gives me a chance to open up to new puppies and share insights on sundry matters.

Now Henry's just about to leave for a four-day tour. This morning he held my ears lovingly and said, "Be up and going fast today. I need to board you at the daycare for four days while I am on this Europe tour. I'll pick you up on Friday, and we'll go to a dog park. 'Til then. You are a nice boy."

I got ready in a jiffy, and Hen boarded me for the next four days. By the time I reached daycare, Loki and Kiko were there already, most probably chatting about me. Luke and Pixie were still missing.

"Is that a breathing haystack walking toward us, or has Mother Nature blessed us with another day of Weekday?" Kiko took the first shot at me even as he was making his way to the ring.

"I am a haystack any old day of the week." I had heard it. And like every time, I was ready to give it back.

"Okay, haystack! How are you?" Kiko poked back at my nose.

"Good, and how are you? And you, Loki boy, wassup?" I greeted back with a grin.

"All sun and stars. How are you this morning?" Loki answered.

"Good, like I said." I looked at the road leading up to the daycare. Luke and Pixie were still not there.

"Where's Luke and Pixie?" Loki asked.

"No sight of them yet." I looked out some more.

While Luke is yet to arrive, I'll tell you a thing or two about him.

Bright, bouncy, and bespoke, Luke is someone who would be friends with Mike Tyson as likely as he'd be with Michaelangelo. Don't we have that one friend who's friends with everyone else in the universe? That's Luke, the Belgian Shepherd in our wolfpack. He does spurt out the odd stupid things now and then. That's a bit of a put-off along with the ever-cursed dog thing of chasing his tail that Luke does almost always when he is bored.

But for all that Luke is and isn't, there's no match for his unadulterated love for adventure. Spread some freshly baked adventure on the table and trust the ever-athletic Loki boy to sniff it from a hundred miles. Speak of the devil . . .

"Hi, Loks. Hey, Kiko, Weekday. How are you guys today?" Luke had arrived.

"All great here," Loki remarked.

"Sup, Luke, late today, eh?" I asked.

"Better late than whatever." Luke seemed a little lost in thought.

Luke the Warmest

Hi! I am Luke, a Belgian Shepherd, and the single greatest quest in life is to find out who gave me that name. I mean, look at Loki. Now that's a cool name. "Luke" is like from the nineteenth century, duh! Plus, being in the same gang with Loki kinda already puts pressure on you for being the second-best name with four letters, two of which are "l" and "k." Thankfully, by sheer merit of personality, I am the warmest guy in the gang, not *lukewarm*, more like the warmest. Nevertheless, that's what I got, and I don't complain a lot about that because F5 is the coolest gang in at least thirty daycare centers I've never visited.

I visit the daycare only occasionally. My story is slightly different from the other four in the gang. I stay with my mom Bella, who's a single mother with a middle-school-going kid. That would be my human sister Lana. Lana and I are the best of friends. It's unbelievable the pace with which she has grown since I first saw her. It's been extra fun being around a growing kid, so much so I can write a book on it. But that's another story for another day, also one's that rewritten a thousand times already.

Right now, I still dream about the days when I was an athlete and took down opponents by the dozens. We'll talk more about that in another minute. It's just a great shame a former champion athlete has to sit watching cartoon shows in the mornings instead of jumping, hopping, galloping, and whatnot. While I never complain about being a TV partner to Lana, frankly, I don't enjoy it either.

If I could change one thing in my life just about now, it would be just about this: mix some play to the party, sonny! Bring in some adventure before it's too late in the night. On second thought, late in the night is just as pretty. The latest daycare discussions that we've been having among the F5 seem to lead into some kind of a different dimension of adventure altogether, but we won't go there just yet. For now, keep those eyes glued to my story.

Long before I came to Lana and Bella, I used to live with David. Like Kiko's dad, David was a former athlete. He later turned into a dog sports trainer. That's putting it mildly. David dedicated his life to training dogs in sports. It was during David's peak as an acclaimed canine athlete trainer that he brought me home. I have very faint memories of the time I came to David's home. But from whatever I can recollect, those early days felt like magic.

I got the best food and sport for any puppy around the country. Moreover, David was one caring dad. Above and beyond being a stern taskmaster, he was a kind man who brought me up like I was his child. It must have been the gentleness and charisma of David that I never got to realize when the innocent puppy play turned into fierce dog sport training. We trained day in and day out, hitting the training grounds, parks, and everything in between. David was obsessed with making me the best in athletics.

Ask any athletic dog, and he'd tell you nothing is as majestic as being admired for skills in sports. Before I could reach my senses, I climbed over a thirty-foot wall like it was a hill of sand. I could jump over ten feet walls a few thousand times a day by the time I was a year old. In addition to nine hours of training every day, my routine involved walks in the park, Frisbee, the occasional pool party, and sometimes hangouts with other pets in the neighborhood. You might find it hard to believe, but once in a blue moon, David also brought me a sugar-free cheesecake!

David sincerely believed I had it in me to be the best athlete in all of dog-verse. To be honest, that came more from a father than from a trainer. I had seen many, many dogs in umpteen competitions to know better, but I believed as long as David believed.

Time flew like a child's paper plane. Before I knew it, we were celebrating my second birthday. There were enough gold trophies in our cupboards to buy us a new home. David and I had won events across the states and were shortly planning a trip to Europe for multiple dog sport events.

While I was sailing over the moon with joy, I knew Europe would not be a cakewalk. Competing with athletes from all around the world wasn't going to be easy. Having lost the first place by a whisker of a second for close to half a dozen times, I knew it better than anyone else.

"You know it's a bit beyond me, don't you?" I asked David one evening after training. I was still struggling to regenerate steady breathing.

"Is it about Europe?" David threw the question back at me.

"Yes, what else?" I drew a long face, quite atypical of me.

"What makes you think so?" David sounded sharp.

"Nothing in particular. We've never been to an international event before. I've never seen a dog from another country before. You know, that feeling of uncertainty." I tried to sound positively confused.

"No, I don't know that feeling. I've never had that feeling when I've seen you train. You never have that feeling when you train. Only when you finish with the training does your mind start ticking and these thoughts seep into your brain. Do you know what that means?" David asked grimly.

"What does that mean?" I was surprised at David's spontaneity.

"That means your mind isn't tired enough from the training!" David said with a hint of a faint giggle in his tone.

"Whoa! Where did that come from?" I said, immediately realizing he'd caught me off guard.

"No, I'm serious." David recollected his composure. "When you train well, your mind becomes thoughtless. You eat your dinner, and you doze right off. You get up in the morning and train again." That was overwhelming spontaneity for a singular conversation in the continuum.

"Wow! So I am not supposed to think." I felt somewhat like a robot following human instructions.

"Yes and no!" the Robocop replied.

"That was enlightening, sir. Would you mind elaborating a bit?" I was more confused than a hummingbird flying backward.

Now why does a hummingbird need to fly backward in the first place? It could just turn around and fly face forward. Isn't it much safer that way? David always said, "Eyes on the target." Why doesn't he train a few hummingbirds, duh?

"I know what you're thinking. That I am treating you like a robot, a thoughtless machine that's not entitled to an opinion." David had this amazing ability to soften his timbre at will.

Did he just read my mind there? I thought to myself.

David continued, "However, it's not that. It's just the thoughts that I want you to keep away. They cloud your vision and lower your intensity.

I still want you to feel the same intensity. As an athlete, the way you feel is always more important than what you think." That was coaching gold. "That's also why you are not a robot either. Machines don't have feelings, remember. They're still useful because they don't have thoughts either." David smiled at me. He'd smile every time after confusing me like that.

"Sometimes you speak more like my trainer than my dad," I couldn't stop myself from saying that.

"Yeah! I know that. But that's not all. We still got to fix that little head of yours and all the magnificent thoughts inside it." David started laughing as he said that.

"How exactly do we do that?" I was all ears.

"Simple. We double the reps in the last hour of your training." I still remember David's straight face when he said that, as if one full hour of doubled reps meant nothing.

"That's insane!" I was all up and alarmed. "That could kill me. You know that!"

"Don't worry, champ. I would never have you do anything that you couldn't ace in a heartbeat." David's confidence in me bathed my existence with joy and anxiety simultaneously.

That night was the last time David's heart beat. He never woke up the next morning. The doctor said he suffered a major cardiac arrest and his heart stopped functioning.

I did not believe the doc. I barked and barked at David. When I was tired, I barked some more. He refused to wake up. I said the emergency code that he'd taught me at least a thousand times. David did not budge. He kept looking the other way even when I tried turning his head with my paws. For a long, long time, I thought he was angry with me for not saying an instant yes to an hour's training with doubled reps. How I wish I'd said yes right then.

I laid my chin on his chest and hoped against hope that he'd just start breathing somehow. An hour went by. Nothing happened. Another hour passed, and more people gathered at our house. I knew they were there for David, and I clung to him as a child clings to his dad.

"Come on, David. They'd take you from me if you don't get up now," I cried to his soul. "Wake up, David. Wake up for me, Dad."

A part of me believed David was playing the dirtiest of pranks on me. He'd pranked me before but never with such closure, never so terminally. That part of me died that day as they took David out of the house in the afternoon. I kept calling out to David. He did not hear me; no one did.

I could tell you how broken, lost, and deprived I felt when I realized David was gone. But no words can describe a child's loss of his father. It's a cold, ruthless void. It's a vacancy that's never filled. All you do is carry that pain in the heart for life and use it as a reminder of the ultimate, irreversible truth.

I never went to Europe, and I never trained after that. Training and David were the same things for me. I trained because David was my trainer. I knew there would be dozens of trainers rallying up to adopt me. But I just did not feel like stepping into the grounds without David. I remember how I always went to bed with anticipatory excitement about training the next day. David had taken that feeling away with him.

Later that afternoon, some lady in the uniform loaded me on a vehicle and took me to a place with many malnourished dogs. I figured all of them had lost their fathers, mothers, brothers, or sisters. From being a champion dog winning event after event without even breaking a sweat, I became just another helpless pup "up for adoption."

As I had gauged, the first to turn up were the trainers, hordes of them. They'd all seen me beat the daylight out of their dogs in events. They all wanted me, not out of a sense of empathy, but simply to snatch the first prize in games. I did not mind all that. Frankly, I just did not care.

At the adoption center, I would look at people and, in one breath, tell if they were trainers. Then I would just not look their way again. The people at the adoption center were kind enough to ask them to leave. They were quick to figure out I did not want to go to a trainer and, after a while, rejected all trainers that came for me.

Then Malcolm came to me. He looked like a middle-aged man consumed by years of loneliness. He gazed at me for a full minute and asked someone at the center if he could take me out for a walk in the yard. They let him take me, and I walked out into the yard, my shoulders drooping down my frame.

"Do you miss him, champ?" Malcolm said softly.

"No, I still feel him around." I thought that would douse his interest in me, and he would go back to nothingness.

"I do too. My dog left me over six years back, and I still feel he is right in front of me." Malcolm looked straight at me and then lowered his gaze as if to hide a tear.

I felt the pain in his voice. It seemed he had lost someone dear too. He hadn't recovered from his loss in all these years. Maybe Malcolm's was the home I was never looking for and was destined to go to anyway. And I did not want to spend the rest of my days in the adoption center. Right then, I trusted Malcolm to be my person for the rest of my life, a mistake I cannot regret enough when I look back at it.

It turned out Malcolm owned and managed the biggest dog-fighting pit in the state. He made me his champion dog. For the next two months, he fed me like I was a dinosaur and injected me with enough hormones to turn a chicken into a bull. I resembled a mini-bull that he took me to the fighting pit.

I remember my first fight like it happened yesterday. My opponent was another Belgian Shepherd, the finest I have ever seen. They called him Luca. He was so majestic that I didn't even remember why. Honestly, I didn't even know what kind of fight I was supposed to fight. Then Luka said, with nothing but plain horror in his voice, "You ready to die, boy?"

"What? Why?" I snapped.

"I'm going to kill you, that's what. And I have no idea too." Luka sounded grave.

"Is all that even necessary?" I was still a little befuddled.

The crowd around the cage grew louder as Luca and I exchanged words. Luca looked at me and growled. The crowd grew madder, to the extent that they started shouting, "Kill, kill!"

I only realized what I was in when I heard the crowd repeat that word as if they meant it. I saw Luca charge at me like a hound in pursuit of his prey. He threw a sturdy right hook. My defenses kicked in timely as I swung low to my left out of pure muscle memory and dodged his paw. I had zero training in fighting. But I had reflexes drilled in by months of athletic training. In a fighting pit, reflexes are invariably powerful.

I could tell you how the rest of the fight went bit by bit. But it suffices to say that the entire battle was like a cat chasing a mouse, with me dodging most of Luka's blows. Being the athlete worked to my advantage. Luka tired pretty soon, and I refused to hit him even once. The match ended in a draw.

That night, I cried myself to sleep. Being pitted against another hound hungry for your blood can be devastating. I couldn't curse myself enough for believing that sly old douche and his sob story. All I could remember was David's face and how he magically transformed into a caring father after each day's training.

Malcolm did not give me any food for three days after that first fight.

That was for not winning him the match. On the fourth day, he lit a fat cigar and told me, "Win me this fight tonight or starve to death."

I fought for my food and for my life too. I won, without feeling guilty for hurting a brother dog. If you judge me for that, here's what I ask you, "When was the last time you literally had to fight to win a meal?"

Over the next several weeks, I won a meal after meal and never slept hungry. Malcolm had picked the apt champion for his pit. Soon enough, winning fights became a habit, like winning athletic events had once become. At first, I did it because I had to. I'd tell myself I was doing it just for my dinner. Then it turned ugly. I got better, and I started enjoying the fights. A lot of it was because no dog had trained like me. No one was so agile, fit, and strong. No one had a David to teach them. Plus, I was all muscular now, courtesy of the God-knows-what hormones Malcolm injected in me.

Malcolm! That son a snitch was making more money than he could ever know how to spend. That and precisely that turned out to be his biggest undoing, not making money, but not knowing how and when to spend it. You see, the authorities take note when you book a vacation villa in Italy, buy a

$150K yacht, request private jet quotes from three aviation companies, and drive home a brand new Porsche—all within a couple of weeks.

Malcolm landed in deep fit (along with that word you first thought of). The police took him to the hospital and then to the lockup. The dogs, including myself, were smuggled off inside some dark truck by Sergio, Malcolm's close aide. That truck, I tell you, just kept traveling. We saw neither food nor light nor water nor the next two days and two nights. Around ten dogs were thirsty, starving, and on the verge of collapsing.

Those two days were peculiarly strange. I did not feel particularly thirsty or hungry or in need of any kind of refreshment. There was just a particular kind of lull after fighting tirelessly for all those nights. It might sound kind of weird coming from a borderline terminally-unfed dog, but an awkward sense of peace had dawned upon me even inside that stinky gray vehicle. Something told me the ordeal was about to end.

We were lost in sleep when Luca barked abruptly. Waking up in a fit, the other dog and myself wondered what could have happened. Then Luca said with a loud growl, "If we want to escape, this is our best chance." Yes, Luka and I were together and had become good friends after that first fight. Malcolm had bought him from his owner. We shared the same room (along with seven other dogs) for the rest of our stay with Malcolm.

"What happened?" some dog asked in a drowsy-sleepy tone.

"The truck stopped, that's what happened!" some other dog replied.

I was still sleepy, while the others were indulging in some dumb pre-death banter.

"For how long have we been still?" I asked lazily as if all of it was just a dream.

"An hour, maybe," Timba, the German Shepherd, replied.

"It's a lot more than that," someone else joined the conversation.

"ONE DAY!" Luka shouted at the top of his pitch. All of us stood up in historic readiness. "The truck hasn't moved in a day." He toned himself down somewhat.

"What the hell?" two or three of us said in unison.

Luka continued, "I am pretty sure the driver ran away at least a day ago. We either make an early move or eat each other for dinner."

Now dogs do superhero stuff when the hour demands saving lives and avoiding being eaten by other dogs for dinner. I was so exhausted then that I could barely recall how we did it. But what I do know is that ten dogs gave it all they had to break open a thick steel latch right from the screws that fastened them to the door.

It was late in the night when we broke out of the truck. It was parked next to an enormous agricultural field. The sky was jet-black with at least a zillion stars sprinkled on the domed pie. That's all we had. It looked a place without a living soul in the next hundred miles. That night we were literally in the middle of nowhere. The only respite came in the form of a little stream. The lot of us drank water like it was the last day before the apocalypse.

"What now?" Timba asked.

"We need to find the road. The truck must have come through some road." I was still slurping on those last drops of water.

"Forget the road. I just found dinner." Luca steamed in from a distance as if he were a galloping horse chasing the finish line.

The big dog had broken into a small cottage and found a massive canister of morning cereal ready to be gobbled up by ten dogs cast away in a desert without sand. That night we didn't even bother looking for some silly road. Heavy bellies, empty heads, grassy fields, stargazing, and hypnotic sleeping took over the rest of the night.

We woke up early the next morning to considerable chaos. Three out of the ten dogs were missing. We figured they must have gone looking for the road. Sure enough, they came back in an hour with news of an extensive highway a few dog miles from the fields. The dog party sped to the road and reached there in about thirty minutes.

The first hour of road watching was rather disappointing. No vehicles and no humans. We had started wondering if the road even saw any car through the day. As daylight broke, we saw a few cars approaching from a distance. The cutest ones among us were in charge of securing a lift on a large vehicle.

It worked. A big, burly, and dog-cuddly guy with a huge truck saw us by the road. The first thing he did was empty at least a dozen packs of biscuits for our breakfast—full marks for the extra cuddling. He loaded us all in the truck and drove away, singing songs about friendship, freedom, and fresh starts.

Six days from that morning, I was in the home of Bella and Lana. The friendly truck fellow left us in the safe company of a dog rescue group, who moved swiftly on their feet to find each of us a permanent home.

Everything inside Lana and Bella's home felt hunky-dory. The fridge was stocked with food, the sofa had foam, and there was surplus entertainment too. I memorized their entire playlist of TV shows in a couple of weeks. After that, it gradually became a drag. If you've experienced race track adrenalin and loaned breaths every night at the fighting pit right after, "couch potato" doesn't sound like a promotion. Imagine Kurt Angle at the peak of his action days, after all the race track laurels and wrestling parked on his couch watching soaps all through the day. Precisely how I felt!

That was six months from this morning. Right now, I need to hurry my bum to the daycare because the mom and daughter are out on a short trip of two days, and there's no food in a house where there's no human.

"Coming!" I shouted to Bella as she revved up the car engine.

The party had already arrived as I entered daycare. Weekday, Loki, and Kiko were already there at the daycare.

"Hi, Loks. Hey, Kiko, Weekday. How are you guys today?" All three of them seemed fresh like daisies.

"All great here," Loki remarked.

"Sup, Luke, late today, eh?" Kiko asked.

"Better late than whatever." My thoughts went back to that night in the field where we earned our freedom.

"All good, Luke! Seen Pixie yet?" Kiko answered.

"No, but I guess she's always the last one to arrive anyway," I said with all honesty.

Well, Pixie. Who doesn't know Pixie? To the uninitiated, the map in our daycare has a legit place called Sassabama, the home of Pixie, the poundful. For a lady that's barely a few pounds of accumulated topsoil, Pixie moves around with some serious oomph. She strongly believes she can see ground-level truth better because of her low center of gravity. The rest of the pack strongly disputes the claim though.

If there's one thing Pixie is good at, it has to be melting humans. She can melt people with her starlike gaze and establish authority over fresh human laps in seven seconds flat.

"All hail the queen of Sassabama, first of her name, annihilator of bubble wraps, seer of ground-level truths, breaker of fridge locks, blocker of balcony views, savior of Jersey College, humiliator of cats, and hater of Zen," Kiko, Loki, Weekday, and I greeted Pixie as she entered.

You got it, and we'd made and memorized that piece of intro just for her. Yes, we sang it every day as queen Mega Pixels walked down the silver pathway.

Mega Pixels

Hey, guys! They call me Pixie. I am a Chihuahua, a professional bubble wrap annihilator, and if you don't know the El Paso Chihuahuas, I am already mildly disappointed in you. Most humans give it their best to win my affection, attention, or sometimes even just a glance. That's where I must pause and tell you I am tough to please, but that's for people in general. Ask my sisters Hannah, Daisy, and Maria, and they'll let you know I am made of pure love. Yes, I share a room with three other young girls; they being humans is mere happenstance.

My hobbies include playing innocent with humans and melting their hearts with my starlike gaze, establishing immediate authority in the new territory of fresh human laps, and gathering intelligence inputs from the outside world. Additionally, I take categorical interest in the most abstract Society for Small Dog Emancipation, musings on effective leadership, collecting intangible pieces of art, torn toys, and leather memorabilia from footwear.

I am not as regular to daycare as Weekday and Kiko. I just pay occasional visits whenever my sisters are busy with exams or outdoor parties. Right of the blue, I share a somewhat bittersweet relationship with that son of a bitch Loki. Among the sons of bitches at daycare, my favorite ones are Kiko, Luke, and Weekday. I can't determine why most humans use that term as an expletive. All my kind are sons and daughters of some bitch or the other. I am not that particular about us "bitches" thrown around as expletives, but yeah, whatever.

My sisters Hannah and Daisy are from Texas, and they're as Texan as they come. I couldn't believe that the two of them had never seen a snowman before coming to Jersey. As for Signorina Maria, she's an international student from Italy. These girls perhaps represent the only collective of three humans that are in relative peace living with one another. For starters, I love all of them like they were my kin. And they treat me like royalty. That doesn't prevent me from being skeptical about their cumulative intelligence.

I often share hackneyed stories about the "profound dumbness" of the girls with Loki, Weekday, Luke, and Kiko. That helps us burst into quick laughs now and then. Like this one time, they brought home a kitten and thought I'd be all blushy and pampering about it. No way! I might be a small dog with cute little steps, but I am not a kitten's toy. Not in this life, not in the next hundred. I did not eat all day, and that son of a catitch slept inside the trash can by the street at night.

If you thought the cat was a one-off thing, let me remind you, there's just no end to human dumbness. On my first birthday, all the girls (including their friends) dressed up in traditional Mexican and thought I'd be over the moon with the stunt. Bonkers! For the longest time, I couldn't figure out what those dresses were. I Googled a bit and took severe offense at the cultural appropriation. Now just because a dog traces her origins back to a nation, it doesn't mean it's born with the history of the place coded in its genes. Silly humanitchs!

Yes, I am a cruel judge of human intelligence. But that doesn't and shouldn't matter once you start pampering me. That's how the girls get away with their atrocious dumbness every frickin' time. The license to my nonjudgmental reciprocation upon pampering is not just limited to your being human. I am equally accommodating for fellow dogs that pamper me. And speaking of incoming pampering from dogs, no one even comes close to the F5. They love and spoil me like I am legitimately from their own family.

If you thought I am done with the self-praising, go to Chihuahua hell. They don't call me the queen of Sassabama for nothing. The singular quality I like most about myself is my nonnegotiable allergy to nonsense. Here's a quick example: The F5 finds it hilarious when I claim that I can see ground-level truths because of my lower center of gravity. Like all the dumb humans, they use it to crack a quick joke about small dogs and how they can't "look up" the right angles. Like duh! Someone go tell them that being small has its advantages. Quick demonstration: I can read this, and you should not: Go to hell!

Just like being small, being the youngest in the gang also has its advantages. I'll tell you the first one right away: A young guy has less experience in the darkness of life. And he is less likely to narrate a tear-jerking story about death, separation, anxiety, and more death. On the contrary, the little life I have lived is all filled with adventures: typical city adventures, the kind you experience when you share life and living room with three young college girls.

This one dates back to last year. It was the last weekend of August. The girls had to do something crazy before the summer ended. Like most humans with poor financial planning, these girls were low on cash around the end of the month. However, not having money was hardly a problem. Not having a plan was one. So they thought and thought hard but arrived nowhere. It was already eight in the evening, and the poor bitches had no idea how to conclude the summer on a high.

Now you don't always need a plan when you're just forty miles off Lower Manhattan. It's generally the other way around—there's a plan that needs you. If four girls in their early twenties are hanging around the bar of a posh NY pub, rest assured some hunky rich dude with a fancy Lamborghini will ask them to join this mad party they're hosting at his house. But that happens only when you reach the place early enough to be spotted by one of those party hunks.

Maria, Hannah, Daisy, and yours truly were awfully late. We reached a somewhat local pub on 9th Avenue at around 11:00 p.m. Despite being so late on a Friday evening, we should still have found sufficient people in and around the pub. But no, there were just a couple of girls. One of them had passed out, and the bar lady was furious with her, blabbering some French in Russian. What? Why?

Nevertheless, we were there and thought we should make the most of whatever we had around us. Technically, the girls thought that, and I just counted myself involuntarily, so they didn't feel like they're forcing their fun on me. Yeah, that's a thing.

Like all weird NY pub tales set on Friday evenings, it began with a few drinks. The girls started chit-chatting among themselves. The first (and rather predictable) thing they talked about was the acute nonexistence of agreeable young men in the pub. Forget agreeable and young. There wasn't a single guy in the vicinity. Something about that fact seemed weirdly problematic.

The conversation quickly switched to which of the girls was going to marry and at what age. Now you know why I make fun of their profound dumbness at the daycare! Sorry, I digress. A few drinks down, the girls broke rank and made short trips to the bathroom. When they came back, there was a kind of calm eeriness permeating through the pub's atmosphere. The staff was all lined up at the entrance as if waiting for Ryan Reynolds to arrive in his Green Lantern suit.

Then he entered the pub—a man, halfway (plus some more) through his age, and in a tall frame. He had a thick salt-and-pepper beard, hazel eyes shining with masculinity, side-parted hair (a bit like George Clooney's), and three distinct lines across his forehead running parallel to his brows. He wore a thick leather jacket that was uncharacteristically heavy for the summer. There was also an unimaginably expensive tan briefcase, the kind that you could throw a glance at and tell forever that it had wads and wads of thick Benjamins inside.

That the man oozed charisma and magnetism by the boatloads would be an enormous understatement. The gentleman looked like he was from another country altogether. I don't just call anyone a gentleman by merely looking at them. Also, it was literally another country. This guy looked the part and after a long, long time, looked like someone who was a real man in the first place. We were bowled over and spell-bounded in equal parts.

Soon enough, the usher escorted him to one of those private "RESERVED" tables.

"Did you girls see that?" Daisy hushed, her eyes were doing all shades of pink in no time.

"Looks Italian." Maria had lost half of her wine-toll already.

"How do you know?" Hannah hushed back.

"I just know. I can smell an Italian guy from ten miles away and store him as an encrypted piece of memory forever," Maria said with her characteristic blush.

"What's that? Is he a spy or something? And a nice piece of mnemonic tech there, Mari!" Daisy pointed out to his table.

The man brought out some kind of sophisticated equipment and placed it on the table. For starters, it looked like a gigantic cell phone. But it had an antenna, the type they use on satellite phones. My curiosity had already blasted through the roof.

All the girls summarily fermented a collective urge to find out everything about this man right then and there. Correction: Two of the girls summarily fermented the call. Maria had already answered the urge. Before we could know, she was all topsy-turvy-ing her way to the man's table. She said something to him in Italian. The man raised his head from his device and looked at Maria. He buzzed a few words, mostly in Italian, and sunk his head down to look at his device again.

Maria returned to the bar, and by the time she had returned to the girls, Mr. Macho Italiano had brought out three other cell phones from his jacket sleeves. I am not kidding, no. This guy had four phones on him, and one of them was a frikkin' satellite phone. And the jacket, that jacket of his, I can't tell you enough about it! It wasn't any regular New York sighting either. And I've seen plenty of New York in my heydays. Just know that James Bond would have paid an arm and a leg to lay hands on a jacket like that.

While I was thinking all that, the trio made a wolf pack and swarmed over to his table. Why would they leave me back for such a critical mission? Weren't we all sisters for life? That day, for the first time in my life, I tasted the bitter ice cream flavor called discrimination! First paw!

Like the girls, my first impressions of the man were those of awesomeness. Then something struck me, something about this cool suave and decisively macho man didn't feel all right. It was just this strange thing I feel in the gut every time I know something is not hunky-dory. There was no hard evidence to back what I felt. I just knew it. But did I know enough to stop the girls? Perhaps no. So I tailed along.

An hour and plenty of flirtatious small talks later, the girls and I were seated in a fancy Rolls Royce limo and were joined by a band of young boys on our way out of the pub. They were playing the latest Drake number and speaking of which ones are going to marry and at what age. Duh!

Just then, I had this strange feeling of eeriness again. It was the peculiar gentleman's sudden silence that struck me hard. His mind was working at a magnificently overclocked frequency. I knew we were heading into trouble of an extremely irreversible manner—straight on and head first. I had to get out of there. That was the natural part. More importantly, I had to get the girls out of there. That was the hard part.

They were way too deep into the "party" to pay attention to any of my small-time tantrums.

I called out to them a couple of times. They pretended that I did not exist inside that mini-resort of a Rolls Royce. That irked me real bad. So I did it for the first time in my life. I rolled over and laid on my back, distributed my limbs in a sort of balanced, antigravity laziness, drew out my tongue, and hung it downward in the air and looked sideways with each eye in the opposite direction.

Yes, I played dead. With a Hollywood-styled death whimper!

The girls took a while to notice. As soon as they did, they raised hell. Now young girls like Maria, Hannah, and Daisy with the fresh freedom of college have peculiar fancies about long limos, fashionable guys, and millionaire men. But the moment they realized their precious li'l Babe X (wrong time to mention, but that's what they call me) is in searing pain and presumably dead, they forgot about the entire frickin' universe.

The limo sped to the nearest vet hospital, and the doc declared I was "brought fit." Nevertheless, I kept playing dead for another full hour, long enough for the naysayers to go home. The moment I realized they were far enough, I got up and, ahem, complained of "exaggerated and prolonged partial chest pain of a nonmedical-book nature." The girls thanked God, and we went home that night.

It wasn't until the next morning that Hannah realized that I'd outright faked it. I told her what I honestly felt, and she told Daisy and Maria. They did not speak to me for three days after that. The FBI arrested a week from that night in the pub a certain runaway Italian criminal called Casimiro Mancini. Charges included smuggling, money laundering, racketeering, and aiding terrorists operating out of the Gulf.

The news was all over the television. The guy they arrested was the chick magnet from the pub, except for the jacket. I am sure he tried to use the jacket to bribe someone and evade it. Too bad, James Bond wasn't the officer in charge.

That wasn't the only time I saved all of us from definitive danger. The other incident I remember rather distinctly was from college. I shouldn't have been there in the first place. My sisters had chosen to study at a college where all pets the size of a "cat" and beyond are not allowed. That is the precise rude rule. But what the profoundly dumb girls keep telling me is this: "Sorry, babe, cats ain't allowed in there."

The college thingy started with Zen, Hannah's ex-boy. When Han was dating him, he came to our place frequently, mostly when Daisy and Maria were out on weekdays. That meant they were in class, and Han was skipping school in favor of romancing what was admittedly a cute guy.

At the time, I had a secret pact with Hannah—not to tell the other girls about Zen coming to our place during the weekdays. Of course, he would visit on the weekends too. But only when all of us were in, he pretended not to know the place at all. The dimwit would twaddle things like "Which way is the bathroom again?"

"Yeah! Right around the corner, where you were helping Hannah dry her hair for a full hour the day before yesterday." I would push to Hannah, who, by the way, has a custom hairdo titled "innocent on weekends."

It is my theory, but I very ardently believe that cute guys and smart girls make terrible couples and vice versa. The cuteness kinds should stick to their game and find others that just do cute. In a mix between cute and smart, it is always the smart ones who end up burning their hearts. Every so often, the cute ones are dumb and insensitive. Add to that the corruption that seeps in with the realization that "cuteness" can be maneuvered to twist the minds and hearts of others. Irredeemable mayhem!

When I know something about you that concerns your well-being, I approach you and tell you about it. So I did with Hannah. I told her with all due reasoning. Her cute boy wouldn't hang around for long. Since she was the smartest of the three girls, I thought she would understand.

"Is Zen cheating on me? Please don't tell me my Zeny honey is cheating on me!" Hannah inserted a scream inside a choke while delivering those lines.

"No! He's not cheating on you. He's just cute. And I just explained to you what follows cute. Can't you see?" I was very disappointed with Hannah.

"No, I can't. Don't. Just don't ever repeat anything like that about Zen." Hannah was weeping by then.

So I stopped right there. I realized the girl ought to learn her lesson the hard way. On a regular day, Hannah was smart enough to know what I was talking about. To quote science writer Rita Carter, "Where thought conflicts emotion, the latter is designed by the neural circuitry in our brains to win." That's science. And science has no business interfering in matters concerning C-U-T-E. Cuteness trumps all.

What Hannah did not understand when I spoke to her that day, she realized later in a manner much more dramatic than it should have been. Owing to my hygiene affinity, I visit the vet biweekly to have the inside of my mouth flossed. It generally happens on Saturdays since the girls are adequately bored on weekends.

On one such weekend, the girls found something interesting to do (don't ask what) and conveniently skipped my floss. The giveaway was Hannah would take me to the vet on Tuesday because she would "anyway work an assignment from home." I am big on punctuality, but I have to give the girls a day or two of grace time when they plead for it. Consider the fact that I was very much a part of that exciting bit on Saturday (again, no one asks what).

Then Tuesday came, and with it came the overlord of cuteness Zen. While he had always been a great fan of mine, I have my reservations about cute boys. They don't sound so pleasant. We'll move over that part. Anyway, the lovebirds were to take me to the vet. We started from home a total of twenty minutes late because, ahem, Hannah's hair was taking too long to dry.

"Babe, can you stay home alone for a couple of hours after the vet, please?" Hannah asked me.

"Umm, why?"

"The paper, I need to finish it at Chelsea's place. I haven't moved a letter on it," Han pleaded.

"Yeah, sure, big deal!" I didn't mind much.

"Thanks, babe, you're such a sweetheart." Hannah beamed. I love her best when she smiles with love at me.

"But why doesn't your cute lady help you with the paper?" I sneered at her.

"If that was about Zen, I am very offended right now!" Hannah said with a wicked smile. By then, she had gotten used to at least some fifty-odd daily jokes on Zenice the menace.

"Don't be, please." I made a cute face. "I love Zen too. Maybe even more than you do," I snidely remarked.

"Now that means war! You know that." Hannah started air-tickling me. That kind of sets my funny bone off. Meh!

The girls and I would often kill time with small talk like that when waiting in the queue at the vet's. Meanwhile, the tooth fairy had gone out to catch some air.

"I wonder, one day, Zen will talk about our future. I don't know why he hasn't done so far." That was my cue.

"Because there is none." I snapped back like the fizz in a beer can. "Yes, he doesn't know enough to think about his future, forget about one with you." I softened my tone.

"That's because he's too young, we are too young." Hannah switched on the defensive mama mode.

"You sounded just like his mother in the first part of the sentence, so you made up the second one quickly."

"Did I now?" Hannah kind of looked into what I had just said.

"Yeah, these things work on a subconscious level, you'll figure. But on the bright side, Zen's with you now. Make hay when the sun dances or whatever!" I put those words out carefully.

"Shines, the sun shines. Make hay while the sun shines," Hannah said with a scornful smile.

"Pixie, you're next!" the vet's attendant called out.

The floss at the vet generally takes about twenty minutes. That day she took over an hour because she said she got an urgent call from home. But I was pretty sure the vet had her cuteness overlord over the phone.

"I think I am late. Chelsea must have started the paper without me!" Hannah twitches her forehead like that when she's freaking out over something.

"Zen, hon, will you please drop Pix home so I can go to Chelsea's place directly from here?" She tried making a cute face.

"Yeah, why not? I can sure do that," Zen said.

"Is that okay with you, babe?" Hannah looked at me with her big green eyes.

"Yeah, cool, I'll go with Zaundice." I put on a fake smile.

"That was a funny one." Zen leaped in an attempt to avoid the insult.

I set off with Zen in his car, and Han took a cab to Chelsea.

"Would you like some ice cream on the way home?" Zen asked politely.

"No need, thanks." I made a straight face.

"Ah, I thought you loved ice cream," Zen came back persuasively.

"No need to impress me. That's what I meant the first time." I gave it back.

"Whoa! That was rude." The sissy oozed out of him.

"Sorry, didn't mean to hurt ya! But I saw what you were doing there," I said calmly.

"I am not trying to impress you. I just asked if you'd like some ice cream." Zen made a that-was-all face.

"You are. And I am not saying you're wrong. I am just saying you're late." I turned toward him.

"Better late than never then. Tell me, Lady Pixie. What can I do for you?" Now Zen was beaming.

"Take me to your college. I always wanted to see my sisters' college." I was all in.

"Ahoy vey! You know the rule about pets at our school, right?"

"Mmm hmm." I nodded.

"You still want to go that way. Hannah tells me you feel very insulted at the allusion about cats." Sissy bro was pegging me hard.

"Yeah, whatever. But you are the one trying to impress here, remember?"

"Gotcha. Not that I need to, but the truth is I am fond of you, li'l Babe X. So yeah, whatever, I'll show you our college. But remember, do not say a word, or they'll set fire on a full year of no studies and great romance." Hmmm, maybe cute sissy wasn't that bad after all.

We quickly fled off to Hannah's college. I pouched myself inside Zen's sack, batpack or catpack, whatever he called that thing.

"There, those are my boys." Zen showed me his gang.

"Hey, Zen, came too early," a gang member was quoted as saying.

"Mo, there's someone I'd like you to meet." Zen reverse-thumbed Mo, pointing toward the catpack.

"Holy grail! You brought a cat . . . Wait, that's a dog. That is a tiny dog. Is that a . . ." Mo seemed curious.

"Yes, I am a Chihuahua!" I yelled at Mo's face.

"I knew it." Mo jumped like a child that's seen a train for the first time.

Eww, that was the fame of Chihuahuas. Yet they didn't allow us to go to the college. Wait, was that a bunnn . . . ny? I had never seen a bunny in my life and always wanted to pet one. And that, right there, was my big opportunity. I didn't realize until I saw some thirty girls scream like they'd seen a monster that I had leaped out of Zen's sack and was chasing the bunny. Oops, bad timing.

In a minute, the word was out that a Chihuahua the size of a cat was trying to seize the campus and take students hostage. No, I didn't mind the kidnapping bit. I've had sleazier crime dreams myself. Why on earth would they say I was the size of a cat? I was much more prominent. Or smaller. But not the size of those peasant cats.

It turned out the college peeps were so thrilled to see me chase a bunny they'd all jumped out of their classes and started rooting for me. And somewhere, amid all that commotion, some son of a hummanitch dialed 911. You heard that—someone 911'd me. The next minute, the campus was swarming with cops. I freaked out—big time. I just could have officially screwed an academic year of Zen.

Then I saw my guardian angels, Daisy and Maria, appeared sprinting out of nowhere, and one of them collected me in her arms. I don't remember which one because I think that was the precise moment I collapsed, more like zoned out. But I remember someone hugging me tightly like I was her child.

That night the girls wouldn't even lose sight of me. Not for the world. The Zen-hen came under a bit of fire from Han. But I told her the truth. That guy could have been all the wrong kinds of cute, but he did nothing to cause arson on campus. Daisy promised she would bring home a bunny. All four of us hugged each other and slept off the night.

When the girls reached college the next day, the campus was swarming with cops, patrol vehicles, metal-detecting equipment, Tasers, and whatnot. When they came chasing after me the previous day, the police had recovered at least three unlicensed firearms from the bushes in the college courtyard.

So they had cordoned off the entire campus and had been ransacking the area ever since. It turned out there were nearly a dozen firearms hidden off at various nooks and crannies on the campus. The next morning the front page of a national daily read, "Major Terrorist Attack Averted in Jersey College; Police Thank Unidentified Chihuahua Hero."

The night the news came out, the girls rechristened me Babe G, where G stands for a "guardian." And that college of theirs, it went from a cat-sized nonsense rule to Chihuahua friendly. Now that's how you reclaim territory, sonny! Daisy tells me they are working on making my statue and planning on inviting me to the ribbon-cutting.

"Cool with that, but Your Highness ain't doing a dang if that's a cat-sized miracle!" That summarily set off a laugh-riot among the girls. And I hear the line rippled through their school, and now everyone wants a piece of me. Lesser mortals, I tell you. Anyway, I am awfully running out of time now. The others must be there already. I can't take any more of those late-coming jibes anymore.

"Hey, Han! You're dropping me to the daycare or what? Do I need to look for a boyfriend now?" Yeah, I am kinda uber-snappy these days.

"Coming in hot, wheels of time at your service, babe." Hannah signaled me to jump in the car. In return, I marked her that my legs aren't that big. So she picked me up like the royalty I am. Time to liberate the daycare of its umpteen voices!

"All hail the queen of Sassabama, first of her name, annihilator of bubble wraps, seer of ground-level truths, breaker of fridge locks, blocker of balcony views, savior of Jersey College, humiliator of cats, and hater of Zen," Kiko, Loki, Luke and Weekday greeted me ceremonially.

You got it. The F5 made and memorized that piece of intro just for me. Ah, how I love these guys!

CHAPTER 2

Daycare Musings

*The real value of this journey isn't in how far we've come
but in how much farther we're willing to go.*

Right as rain, looks like someone's through with all the tales from the F5 members. That also means a successful entry into the daycare. So congratulations are in order. But hold tight because what comes next is not merely entertaining—it's unprecedented. Much of what's about to come starts right here at the daycare. This is the place where the F5 met one another for the first time.

From the outside, the daycare does not look or feel any different from most other commercial establishments. It's nestled amid a whole lot of green in Central Jersey and looks a bit like a small school building, with a large lawn and a substantial central unit right in front of the yard, which, by the way, wears thick snow during the winters—just the way our dogs like it.

The play area has two parts, one for the smaller and another for the bigger dogs. The small and large dogs generally stick to their play areas. But not Pixie—she'll jolly well hang out with the bigger dogs, albeit mostly surrounded by others in the F5.

On a busy day, the daycare buzzes with over seventy dogs. And on most nights, around sixty dogs stay boarded. While some dogs visit the daycare regularly, most others are occasional guests.

What strikes the most to both dogs and dog parents in the daycare is the neat compartmentalization of the daycare. For example, attached to the large outdoor play area is a latched exit where they dump dog waste. There are cages for small dogs and larger cages for bigger dogs. Wait on. There are also executive rooms for families that could afford them. And if you are fortunate with wealthy parents, they could book you one of those swanky suites.

Charges at the daycare could rocket up to $30 a day and boarding starts at $50 a night. That's about how much a family of four humans pay at a motel. You see, humans need clean towels, white sheets, toothpaste, toothbrushes, happy hours, dinner tables, and parking space against every cent of the money they pay. And the dogs, they just need a room—no toothpaste, toothbrushes, bedsheets, towels, or mirrors. They were even billed for a bath separately. Hold on, there's more!

The best part is, unlike humans, dogs do not get to crawl up the Internet and write negative reviews or badmouth about the daycare in their social circles! Given the odd chance they do indulge in badmouthing, it is always the humans that make the call on choosing a daycare.

But not everything about daycare is grim and expensive. The F5 first met at the daycare. They bonded at the daycare. It was at the daycare that they discovered the beauty of companionship. Considering relationships cannot be measured with money, you could say the expense was worth it and then some more. Let us then quickly zoom inside the daycare and lay our ears on some F5 chatter.

"All that rhyme aside, I couldn't have thanked Dad enough for bringing me to this place," Kiko said obsessively.

"You better believe me, I never thought dogs could have nonhuman friends before I saw the lot of ya!" Loki couldn't hide how thankful he was for having made new dog friends.

The F5 would often thank their humans for bringing them to the daycare in the first place. There was a time when the F5 were younger, and their humans had to drag them to the daycare as they cried and whimpered. But look at them now—each dog looks forward to coming to the daycare, especially our F5 heroes. They just can't wait to see one another again, even though all five of them are quite reluctant to admit it.

Leading up to the daycare, every dog had lived their own story. From here on, they could all be traveling the same journey and setting the same course. You'll appreciate the fact that they all had a unique beginning. Much of that came to light when Weekday broke into one of his trademark rants about—take a wild guess—the meaning of life.

"Like I was saying, life starts at the discovery of hope." Weekday recollected some stray thoughts and tried to assign some order to them.

"What d'ya mean 'discovery of hope'?" Kiko was confused.

"Yeah, geniyo! Care to break that down for your lesser colleagues?" Luke was riled up too.

"I am saying this: Until the day you discover hope, you simply live because you're not dead." Weekday made the first attempt at rephrasing himself.

"Weren't that enlightening, fellas?" Pixie seemed to suggest that Weekday's attempt did not mean much.

"Hear me out, lady. Let me ask you this: Don't you all hope to be loved by your humans when you go back home from daycare today?" Weekday wasn't going to give up easily.

"Not really. I mean, not that we do not want love. But I do not hope for love to come in my general direction. We all know they'd love us when we go back," Loki stated the obvious. He still wasn't sure why they were having that discussion in the first place.

"That's precisely my point. You say that because you've not known anything except love so far." Weekday immediately struck a chord with his friends.

"Maybe. But isn't that the same for each one of us?" Loki said in an open-and-shut tone.

"Sorry for the interruption, guys. Am I missing something here? What exactly is the point of this conversation?" said Pixie the poundful.

"Valid question. If you can give me a couple of minutes of undivided attention, I can make this enjoyable for you." Weekday dug in a bit further.

"Oki, I'm in." Loki signed up for the class.

"So are we." Everyone else followed cue.

"Small Chihuahua request coming in. Make it quick, please." That was Pixie again.

"I'm telling you the story of my mom today because it's a story that needs to be shared. Maybe, just maybe, some of you might even be able to relate to it. I have told you all about how Mom left us and how it left everyone, including Henry and Sylvia, distraught with grief." Weekday lowered his voice. "I guess I haven't told you about how Mom came to Henry and Sylvia. She wasn't born at their home." Weekday looked up for a second. Then he looked down again.

"What? Did she switch homes? That's so unprofessional," Pixie blurted with arrogance. Everyone became silent. "Umm, I am sorry. That came out wrong." Pixie could have been wrong, but that did not mean she was devoid of grace.

"Will ya let the old man speak? Where did she come from, Weeko?" Kiko started at Pixie.

"A rescue center," Weekday passively answered. A collective gasp ran through his friends.

"You mean one of those places where they bring sick dogs for treatment and find them a home later?" Loki had to ask right then.

"Yes. The rescue people brought her when she was all of two weeks old—all bones, covered in mud, matted coat, and severely ill. When the vet first saw her, he said she wouldn't make it. She'd given up on any hope of surviving and was so wasted she couldn't even think of having a life ahead. Then it came to her . . ." Weekday paused as it had come to him too.

"Help?" Pixie asked.

"No, hope," Kiko answered.

"Yes. Someone bathed Mom for the first time. She suddenly felt hungry and thirsty all over again. She tried to stand on her paws and walked a couple of steps. The people around her suddenly became all bubbly with happiness and even rooted for her recovery. Then she collapsed. She didn't know when she woke up after that. But she had made an observation she needed to make—they became happy when she tried to walk. And she hoped that she would be able to make them happy again." Weekday's eyes lit up as he was speaking.

As the conversation continued, a strange kind of silence permeated the entire space.

"I think that was what . . ." Weekday resumed after clearing his throat.

"I am sorry, old boy. I just realized how grateful I am for the life I have lived," Pixie cut Weekday in the middle of his line.

The narrative quickly spiraled out of Weekday, and before long, each F5 member started narrating their individual stories. Never mind the fact that they had shared their stories a dozen times already.

Pixie was in the middle of describing how she once punished a band of bunnies for being rude with her girls when something strange struck Loki.

"Did I ever tell you guys the story of how I came to my home?" Loki turned a new leaf.

"Not to me nor anyone else here." Kiko sensed an opportunity to get under Loki's skin.

"Now I come to think of it, and I do know a bit about how Loki came to his parents. Come on, Loks, tell them all about it. For starters, Loki came to first-time dog parents, who are conservative Hindus. They love Loki so much, they even gave him a car of his own. But when Loki first came home, his family had a tough time taking him in. Ain't that right, Lok boy?" Pixie rued.

"Hold it, Pixel. Can we hear more about that from the man himself?"

"No, I don't want to. It won't interest you guys. I mean, it's kinda dull, whatever I remember." Loki seemed adamant about non-divulgence of information.

"Tell us about it, Loki. We insist." Weekday was the first to plead.

"Really! Is everyone in this one?" Loki gauged at the public mood.

"Betcha, we are all ears. No, literally. look at our ears!" Luke literally pointed toward his years.

"Hunky-dory then, laugh anytime you guys feel like it, I ain't minding that. I can't tell you with all my certainty how veritable this one is. But I have this picture in my mind. It has me, my mother, and my siblings." Loki sounded barely real.

"You are talking about those same dreams that keep coming to you, aren't you? How often have you had those dreams of late?" Kiko discovered the link.

"Yes, them. I don't know how many though. The moment is essentially what the movies sell as the happy dog-and-pup moment. I was suckling on my mother's nipples. Or so I thought. Most probably, my siblings were there too. There were other new pups around as well. But some strange sense of recognition told me they were not from my mother. What I can tell you with total certainty is I was super hungry and thirsty too. That totally could have been the first day of my life. I was about to suckle that first drop of milk from my mother. I had made the pull with all my mouth—my little jaws, tongue, and teeth. But the milk stream hadn't arrived inside my mouth. You know I am talking about that millisecond of a gap between the two events. That's when it happened. Like a snap." Loki went from excited to mildly disappointed while delivering that.

"Snap what?" Kiko acted as if she'd woken up in the middle of her sleep.

"I don't know. I was pulled from my mother by some strong and strange force. I guided my little paws toward her. But the force was all too great. Whatever the thing was, it clutched around my core and back and pulled me with such magnificent force. I can't tell you enough about it." Loki struggled to breathe between his words; there was too much tension in his voice.

"Unreal! Every time I hear it, it sounds impossible!" Pixie exclaimed.

"Tell me that's not true!" Luke seemed equally stunned.

"I wish it wasn't so." Loki was just confused.

"What happened then?" Weekday asked softly.

"I lost most of it. I just remember something getting hold of me and pulling me back like some cruel spell of cursed magic. Then I remember chewing on something sweet and passing out. In between those two events, my teensy little paws reached out for my mom. Did she reach out for me too? There's no way for me to know!"

"Aww! I am so, so moved right now," Luke said in a wet voice.

"You have no idea of what pulled you, Lok?" Weekday tried to jog Loki's memory.

"Yes! For heaven's sake, why?" Pixie was more into the plausibility of the act.

"Believe me, I remember two things clearly: First, I was suckling on my mom. Then something disastrous gravity pulled me back. Shortly after eating whatever it was that they fed me, I dozed off. My eyes were moist. Maybe something in me already knew that was the last time I was near my mom. The air around that place had turned dense with cruelty." Loki hopelessly looked up toward the sky.

"Oh! My tiny. I can't fathom what that must have felt like. Wait, what? Are you weeping, big boy?" Pixie couldn't relate to Loki's story. But she was undoubtedly moved by it.

"All I have in the name of my mother's memory are the faintest of smells and the daintiest of touches. I vaguely smelled her and, maybe I remember some of it. Or perhaps not. I can't tell. It's just the softness of her furs that rests somewhere deep inside my paws. Beyond that, there's nothing in me from the dog that brought me into this world. Something very, very cruel stole my mother from me," Loki sobbed, trying to complete his words.

"And robbed you of your natural childhood thereof. How cruel of whoever!" Kiko fumed at fate and whoever else was responsible for Loki's misery.

"Too bad, only a few lucky dogs like me escape such cruelty," Weekday empathized with Loki, dismally realizing how lucky he'd been to have a dog family.

"Why do you think your eyes were moist, Loks? Like, did you know what was about to come?" Pixie placed her paw on Loki's and gently hugged his leg.

"I don't know. I think I wanted to touch my mother and be with my siblings. Again, I am not sure if I had a sense of family, but I knew I was about to be taken away from something invaluable." Loki tried to recover, even as his voice was still wet.

"What happened next?" Luke quipped, placing his paw on Loki's shoulder.

"Soon after that, I became unconscious. The mill must have put me in a crate and then in a van. Because when I woke up, that's where I found myself. And boy, did that thing move or what? It kept moving and moving and never stopped."

"Did you wake up while you were in the van?" Weekday asked Loki, even though he did not want to miss out on details, however uncomfortable.

"That's how I knew I was still alive because I felt the van move. And it kept on moving for a long time even after I had gotten up." Loki emptied whatever remained in that box of memories.

"What did you see around you?" Pixie asked.

"I felt what confusion looks like, big time! Since I had no eyes pop on me back then, all I could do was feel the world with touch, sound, and smell. Nothing made sense, nothing at all. I could hear soft whimpers and scratch from other pups. There was the occasional jerking of the van, two humans in the front seats, birds chirping somewhere out there, different strange sounds from outside the van, maybe even stars in the sky, and the ever-widening distance between Mom and me. I still can't add up what was happening there, even after so many years," Loki rued dispassionately.

"What happened then? Where did you go?" Kiko was unforgivingly curious.

"They put me up at a place that was dark, stinky, and full of hopelessness. There was poop and piss all around my cage, and the stench of it made me feel dizzy. It wasn't until the first couple of days that I discovered it was a puppy store." Something steely took over Loki as he spoke.

"What is a puppy store? Is it where they sell us to humans?" Someone wanted quick answers.

"You said it. A puppy store is where they keep us in cages and display to buyers," Loki said, looking at his claws.

"By buyers, you mean the future families of dogs?" Luke said something comforting at last.

"Take this with a pinch of salt, but most of our families were once our buyers." Weekday was quick to subtract the comfort out of Luke's words.

"No way you want to remind us of that, Weeko," Luke protested.

While Luke and Weekday were going at it, Loki became strangely silent. He was wondering why he was even speaking about those things. He had been making silent promises to himself that he would never let anyone know of those things. Maybe that's the thing about having friends. You end up sharing things you never thought you could.

"Do you remember the puppy store?" Pixie simultaneously interrupted Loki's thoughts and Luke and Weekday's banter.

"Yes, all of it. I remember every bit as if it happened yesterday. But I am not sure I want to tell you guys all about it. I guess I have depressed you enough already." Loki stepped back a couple of steps.

"Who else would you tell, Loki? We are the only people you have." Kiko tickled around Loki's ribs with her nose.

"Now go ahead and tell us what this store was all about." Pixie sprung back in action and tried hard to jump up to Loki's eye line.

"All right. I don't know where to start the puppy-store story. There were two rows of cages facing each other and an aisle in between for humans to walk and watch out for the pups. Where they kept me, I could not see all the pups. But I could hear other puppies around me. There were two puppies, one on each side of me. They were a bit older than me. So they had seen more of the store. It was from them I learned that puppies that are taller and with sharper teeth made the most of the stinky store hospitality. They weren't seen as pretty enough for humans to lap them up. When I had come, there were also three puppies to my front, on the opposite aisle. They must have been cute and little with small teeth. Because the next morning, they were gone." Loki brought out the conjurer's "trick successful" expression with the last line.

"That's so mean," Kiko cried foul.

"Don't stop, tell us more." Pixie speared into Loki's neck and crashed near his front limbs.

"Everything else was just darkness, or maybe it was just that I didn't even have my eyes pop on me back then. Someone would leave a bowl of cereal twice a day, and that was all. I was effectively alone since the first day of my birth, all mired in unadulterated dog excrement." Loki looked the other way.

"That must have been so hard on you. No pup should ever have to bear the brunt of something like that," Luke said, his voice brimming with compassion and fraternity.

"That must have been painful. We feel so sorry for you," Weekday pitched in balmily.

"Don't even remind me about the pain. My heart would swell up, even at the thought of my family. I didn't even know if my siblings were there at the puppy store with me. Nobody showed them to me. I remember how I would whine during the days and weep through the nights. It continued like that for many days and many nights, and then something strange happened." Loki went from hopelessness to a sudden frame of thrill. It was as if something bright had fired up his imagination.

"What happened?" Pixie couldn't control her excitement at the chance of hearing something positive after all.

"A few people came around the aisle. And bam! The pup right across the aisle was gone." Loki made a long face.

"Oy vey! Where did she go?" Kiko was surprised. Or she wasn't and just acted that way.

"Sold, she was sold." Loki made a straight sell.

"Just like that?" Luke was baffled. There was no way he could have faked that.

"Yeah, just like that," Loki confessed.

"Tell us more about it." Luke didn't seem satisfied.

"Every day little kids would come with their parents to the puppy store. They would throw a good look around, carefully check each pup, and get blown away at how seemingly excited the animal was to see them. That was for most kids that came to the store. There were some dumb ones too. They just sat on the fence sour about how they didn't like any of the pups in the store." Loki might well have surprised himself with the detail with which he remembered puppy store things.

"That baffles me, all right," Weekday called out his lack of understanding of Loki's experience.

That Weekday was baffled at what he had just heard said a lot about how grim things must have been. If anything, he wasn't your regular "cute" dog that got worked up with stray depictions of supposedly un-dogly places.

"I don't know why this interests me. But what happens once a kid likes a pup?" Pixie came back at Loki with reinforced enthusiasm. She craved for answers so desperately, Loki knew she would not go home if he did not give them to her.

"Once a kid likes a pup, the usher's eyes light up. The pup is taken out of the cage and sent to 'play' in the play area. Honestly, that is about the first time many puppies experience a touch of love from any other species, from someone that's not a dog." Loki carefully examined the expressions on the faces of his friends.

"Sounds like something to me. I've played with kids. They're the sweetest humans out there," Kiko remarked with zeal.

"Yep. You can say that again. But not all kids are okay with puppies. Some gel along like butter on a hot pan, some others are a bit apprehensive of dogs. So they take more time. But the kids come secondary. The pups are enthralled to touch the ground after days and sometimes even weeks. I remember myself jumping like a hare when I first touched the ground. The store people use that to market all pups as 'playful and active.' If that clicks and, of course, if the kids like, the parents buy. A sale is accomplished." Loki delivered a masterclass in marketing just like that.

"How many times were you shown to humans?" Weekday followed up with another. The query bug seemed to have struck Loki's friends hard on their heads.

"At least once a day over three months and twice or thrice on the weekends. Huskies are bigger dogs, even when they are puppies. And not many people like bigger dogs. Even those who like more muscle on dogs, go for the ones that don't shed. Also, stores mark up the prices significantly on huskies and some other breeds," Loki threw in some more technicality.

"I saw that coming." Kiko knew something was fishy.

"That is why huskies often spend the longest time at the puppy stores and even rescue centers." Weekday ground his teeth with contempt.

"Who came for you finally?" Luke was succinctly looking for a way to close the loop as soon as it could be made possible.

"Someone did, but that wasn't a human. It was another husky. I just had a very vague sense of vision by then. She was the first dog I saw. And boy! Was she pretty or what! Honestly, I made the first real effort to look at another dog after I heard her whimpers. She was all dainty and mild." Loki's voice softened as he spoke, like he'd discovered hope at the end of the tunnel.

"Ahoy! Did she see you too?" Pixie was finally cheered up about something.

"No, she hadn't opened her eyes back then. I think she was barely a couple of days old, most probably taken from her mother and siblings just like they took me. She was in the crate right opposite to me, the one from where the other pup had magically disappeared." Loki giggled within himself.

"Did ya speak to her?" Kiko asked with definitive urgency, evidently embarrassing Loki.

"I said nothing on her first day. I imagined she would be too distraught. But on the second day, I called out to her . . ."

*   *   *

"Hey," I said.

"Can you hear me? I am here, right in front of you," I said in a hushed voice wary of the store attendants hearing me speak to another dog.

"Me! Are you speaking to me?" she asked after a while.

"Yes, I am speaking to you. I am a husky like you. Do you remember where you came from? Or where is your family?" I nudged her some more.

"No, I don't know my place. I don't even know my name. I just miss my mother." She broke down and started crying.

"Don't weep. It's all right. Eat the food," I told her.

"Where's the food? I am hungry." Evidently, she could not locate the bowl right next to her.

"There, on the bowl to your left. Sorry, to your right," I tried to signal the direction with my paws only to realize that she cannot see me. "There's also some water on your right. Can you hear me?" I realized she had dozed off. Maybe she collapsed out of weakness. I was worried she would not make it without food or water. I whimpered loudly enough to attract the store attendants, and one of them saw her and sprayed some water on her.

*   *   *

Loki's friends could barely catch up with the pace and details of the story. Pixie was about to jump into another question when Loki resumed his blank-stare monologue.

"We haven't spoken ever since that day. Since we didn't have any names back then, she called me L, and I called her V." Loki broke down into a hopeless smile as he mentioned her name for the first time before his friends.

"I see where that went. Did you like really lo . . ." Luke was about to venture into the territory of nothingness.

"Yes, I did, and V did too. For two months, we spoke to no one but each other. We never played together and didn't even touch each other because they would never take two dogs out at the same time. I badly wished to play with her. Maybe I still wish." Loki looked at the faces of his friends to see if they were still interested. Yes, they were—they hadn't even been blinking.

"This is stressing me out." Kiko resisted the suspense. "Did you guys ever meet outside of your cages?" she asked.

"No, we did not. I wish I could tell you a sweeter story, but we never so much as shook our paws. We hoped and prayed to God that someone would take us both to the same house. A few days after that, a family bought two small dogs together, and we became even more hopeful." Loki paused for a breath.

"I see where that went as well. Can't feel sorry enough, Loks." Luke moved a little farther from Loki.

"It was after two months that I met her. A family came and took her, just her. I saw her as they took her away. I saw her leave. We did not speak before she left. She just looked at me, her eyes brimming with magic liquid. Those eyes summarized all that we had spoken about in the past weeks. There was love in those eyes. With love, there was betrayal, a mild sense of it. Was there any promise too? I don't know. But there was pain, lots of it. Right then, I told myself that I would seek her. No, I didn't just say, I pledged." Loki created a little room for himself and sank into the grass.

"Why did she leave just like that? Did she not love you too? Did you not call out to her?" Pixie went into a frenzy as she spun herself all over the place.

"It's not that easy, Pixel! She had no other option. We had that discussion between us for at least a hundred times. We both wanted to leave that stinky showcase of a puppy store. What hurt was the suddenness with which all that happened. We never discussed that. I barked at her and kept crying as she left. She did not look back at me." Loki turned his face away from his friends; he did not want them to see his tears.

"Maybe she couldn't look at you like that." Kiko tried to turn him back toward his friends.

"Maybe she didn't believe the way I believed. Maybe she didn't love the way I did. Perhaps she didn't hope the way I did," Loki said as Kiko wiped off his tears. "The weeks after V left me were the worst. I was living in the store like a fish lives inside an aquarium, only because you have nowhere else to go. I would eat, sleep, and pretend to play when they took me out of the cage. I'd lost mom on the day of my birth, then I lost V too. They might as well have named me Loss instead of Loki." Loki sighed.

"Poor you, Loks. We wish we were there for you." Pixie patted Loki on his shoulder.

"I had even given up hope on anyone adopting me. Then like all things in the universe, it changed." Loki looked at Pixie, who looked back at him with her starlike gaze.

"What happened?" Weekday was curious about anything that concerned change.

"A couple came with their son and daughter, and it was the daughter's birthday later that week. So one of us was about to get super lucky." Loki's eyes would sparkle whenever he thought of that moment.

"I am all ears, brother. What happened after that?" Luke reciprocated Loki's enthusiasm.

"Right, so Vishnu and Savitri came with their children Sam and Lakshmi, and it was Lakshmi's birthday later that week. No prizes for guessing, the girl wanted a puppy on her birthday like so many other kids. At that moment, each cage was a temple, church, and mosque. I kid you not, the volume of prayers each of us said inside every cage could baptize all kids in the universe." The sparkle in Loki's eyes slowly expanded to fill his face with energy and hope.

"And save our missionaries millions!" Kiko couldn't let that pass.

"Amid all our nervous prayers, we were waiting to see who the children pick, who they play with, and ultimately, who they like. At first, they asked the store owner to show them some cute lap dogs. I cannot tell you in common parlance how much I hated lapdogs by then. At any rate, they were a total nightmare for high-billed pieces like me. And it happened all the time, every single day." Loki lost half that energy from his face. He shook himself a little and looked back at his friends.

"Did they pick a lap dog then?" Weekday poked at Loki mischievously.

"No, worse. They picked two." Loki fought humor back with humor.

"Oh bad! Did they buy 'em?" Pixie countered.

"Bonkers, they didn't. As they played with the two pups, I saw a feeling of mild disappointment in Sam's eyes. He left his sister to play with the dogs and walked up the aisle again. He threw a brief look at me and walked ahead a few paces. Disgruntled, I placed my chin on the floor. Shortly after, he came back and looked at me again. I saw his eyes—big, black, and full of hope. I'd never seen a pair of human eyes speak so much in so little time. He looked straight into my eyes, and I stood right there—in the stillness of mild hypnosis. My eyes widened, and I just kept looking at him and he, at me. I do not know what happened between us in those few seconds. But one thing became clear to me: Sam was my family, and his family was mine. Sam looked around for an attendant and asked him to place me in his lap." Loki didn't realize when he had closed his eyes and sat down just like a pup while narrating that bit, almost as if he could play that clip in his head at will.

"That! That's where it starts. When your human laps you up for the first time," Kiko sprang in excitement.

"Tell us, Loki, how did it feel?" Pixie was equally stoked until the point she spotted something incredibly nosy.

"Oh, Spark! Is that you? Long time! How have you been?" Pixie said with a straight, inanimate face.

"Hey, guys! Sorry if I am interrupting. I just thought I'd drop by for a quick hello." Spark tried to act smart.

"Not at all, Spark! You're always welcome at the F5." Luke always seemed to have a soft corner for Spark for some inexplicable reason.

"While we can't go F6 because of registration and trademark issues, always remember the F5 counts you in as a family," Loki added to Luke's niceness, albeit with considerable sameness.

"Thanks for the hospitality, guys. That means a lot. But I was wondering why you guys are still hanging around here." Spark wore a quizzical expression.

"Oh! We thought you knew it—there's an apocalypse everywhere else. Only this part of the daycare the Red Cross marked safe." Pixie went from unimpressed to ballistic.

"Good one there, Pixo. I was talking about Julia. She's here at the daycare, and every other homie is lining up to say hello to her." Spark had his tongue out in the air when he mentioned Julia.

"Really! Good for the homies! But who's Julia?" That was Kiko's turn to go ballistic.

"Yeah, who's that? Never heard that name around here? That new homie, Spark?" Pixie was short of words to ask Spark to leave without making him feel weak.

"No, no. Heck no. Julia is the winner of TAGROK!" Spark was just as excited as Loki was a few moments back.

"You mean the Transatlantic Grooming Kontest with a K." Kiko might have sounded mildly excited about that.

"That's the one. Julia is on a nationwide tour of daycare centers. She says she wants to inspire a million other dogs to be as well-groomed as her. Oh, I am so excited. She even hugged me." Spark looked like a fanboy that was about to hit the floor, hazed in bewilderment.

"We are so happy for you, Spark." Luke couldn't care less for Spark or for Julia for that matter. Beauty pageants have little value for those who've been to war.

"Thank you, thank you. But wouldn't you guys want to meet her too? Like, I don't mean to exaggerate, but she is true royalty. Everyone at the daycare is crazy about catching a glimpse." Spark couldn't comprehend why everyone else wasn't as excited about Julia as he was.

"Umm, we don't mean to disappoint. But the F5 will give her a pass." Loki cordially asked Spark to retire for the day.

"What? Why?" Spark was at his wit's end.

"Don't misinterpret us, please. We are more than happy to say hello if Julia or whoever she is visits us back here. But at the F5, we are fangirls and fanboys of the F5 only." Kiko gave Spark a short but accurate glance of how underrated ego wars were between celebrities.

"But let that not disappoint you, fanboy." Pixie could just have buried Spark's head inside a tin can.

"Yeah! By all means, you go to town about Miss Julia of TAGROK fame. You could also say she has the F5's backing if that helps with the approval ratings or something. We don't mind an inch." Weekday gave the celeb-ego thing a little more stretch.

"Sure, I'll be back with the caucuses. Thanks for having me, you guys are the best. I'll pop by again tomorrow if you have me." Spark was as cute as he was dumb. But he was stupid, nonetheless.

"Bye, Spark. We'll have you anytime!" Kiko formally wrapped up the stupidity.

"Can you believe that, Kiko? Yet another fanboy of a TAGROK chick! I am so, so done with this stuff." Pixie threw an immaculate tantrum.

"Say that again, sis. That is now as boring as despicable. We seriously underappreciate our tolerance for this stuff." Kiko patted Pixie on her back.

"But we must not let any of this get under our skins. Remember, brothers and sisters, we are the F5—funky, formidable, fashionable, frequent, and just about any other fancy word that starts with F," Weekday signed off the grand self-congratulation ceremony.

"Yeah, all hail the futuristic F5!" Loki beamed.

"How about Fantastic 5!" Kiko leaned.

"No! No, no, no. You did not do that!" Pixie screamed.

"Oh, I just did!" Kiko gleaned.

"Let me be clear about this, without offending anyone, of course— we cannot afford to be even mildly plagiaristic about this!" Luke was particular about names like fighters are about their signature moves.

"Umm, aren't we guilty already? Like, there is the Fantastic Four, all right!" Pixie had a point.

"Yeah, guilty. But they are F4, and we are the F5. We are guilty, but we are stronger. And like it's happened so many times throughout history, strength overpowers guilt." Loki could, at times, make even dead timber sound reasonable.

"Don't think we can argue with that. But weren't we talking about how Loki got his tail in that big fancy home of his?" Weekday just realized how far they'd drifted midway through the conversation.

"Yes, Loks! Go on. We are all waiting for you." Kiko was the next to catch on.

"I wish I could tell you exactly how it felt to be there. I just don't know what words describe that feeling. Humans in the store had lifted me before. But when Sam lifted me, that was the first time I knew of the warmth of a human's lap. Within a space of ten seconds, I had traveled from utter disappointment to pure bliss." Loki summarily summoned the bliss back on his face.

"Did the others in the family lap you too?" Weekday took after Loki's excitement.

"Umm, not exactly. But Sam and Lakshmi did take me to the play area and played with me for a while. They were pretty sure I was the baby brother they wanted to take home. I was all leaping and pacing up. For the first time in life, I was playing, like really playing." Loki stood up and started moving around. "Meanwhile, Vishnu and Lakshmi still had two left feet each. They were talking about all kinds of things—how tall and big I would grow and how much I would shed. What if I happen to bite a guest? I was pretty disheartened at that because if they found out how much huskies shed, they would never want me around the rugs in their home," Loki relieved a synopsis of the tension.

"Oh poor, poor boy! Did they not agree to take you home?" Pixie played around a little this time.

"You don't have a ton of social media memes about supportive siblings for nothing. Sam and Lakshmi fought for me. Like The Rock would tell you, you win when you fight with your family." Loki couldn't love his older siblings enough.

"Didn't he also say something on the lines of 'Don't worry about being the next me, be the first you'?" Kiko knew more about human athletes than she knew about her kind.

"Not on those lines. The Rock had said just that. One heck of a movie, though, *Fighting with My Family*," Weekday concurred with Kiko's emotions.

"We digress again. How did Vishnu and Savitri come to agree?" Luke kept bringing the others back to the fold of the original discussion.

"They had to. You know, your brother has those eyes to melt stone into the wax. They were still humans. They paid some money to the store owner like they must have done on some of Lakshmi's previous birthdays to buy her soft days. They said they would pick me up in another three days on Lakshmi's birthday." Loki's voice softened.

"Were you happy, pal? Or did you have that strange feeling in your stomach?" Pixie discovered a strange sense of comfort in Loki's happiness.

"A mix of both but mostly happy. I was glad to leave the cage behind, and that brought in considerable relief." Loki set in a tone of quiescence.

"That's relatable. What were you not so glad about?" Weekday pulled at Loki's string of nostalgia.

"Dogs are dogs. We get attached to places and people, regardless of how angelic or horrible they are. Besides, I had found my angel at that place. She was long gone, but the store was the only memory I had of her. Ciao to the store would frankly mean *bella ciao* for V and me," Loki attempted explaining his dilemma.

"I knew it. Sacrifice, there's always a sacrifice! Did they come back on Lakshmi's birthday?" Weekday was hounding after details like a crime investigator.

"Yes, Lakshmi and Dad came to pick me up on her birthday. Here, I must throw in some insight into how they upsell in puppy sale stores. The day you come to pick up a dog, they offer you a range of accompaniments—a cage, a small tote because you're cute, new toys. After all, you want your dog to like you and whatnot. Dad and Lakshmi were nice enough to buy some toys and gullible enough to get that cage." Loki lifted a paw off the grass to mark the height of the cage.

"I knew it, I knew it. The humans always go for the cage." Pixie surrounded herself with an air of ceremonious sanctimony. "You could have skipped that part. We already know enough about your cars," she threw at Loki.

"Anyway, that is where the real fun started. I gently leaped into Lakshmi's lap. Dad began to drive, and Lakshmi sat with me on the front seat. As Dad drove, I felt the breeze on my face. Goodness, it was heaven and a half times better than the stinky van in which they brought us to the daycare. Bring me more of that wind in the face and some of that view too. I jumped and paced in Lakshmi's arms. She freaked out, big time. That is why all first-time dog owners ought to keep their new dog in the trunk. If you show a dog the world on the outside, expect them to put up a bit of a show." Loki sounded handsomely quirky. "Lakshmi told Dad she could not contain me. 'Contain,' mind the choice of word there. Next thing you know, Dad was holding me tight with both of his arms wrapped around me, and Laks was driving the car. After thirty-five minutes of fresh air and some tight shadow-hugging, we reached home," Loki continued like a storyteller for little children.

"How was home like?" Luke asked.

"As Mom heard our car approach the driveway, she opened the door. The first time I looked at that house, my jaw dropped on the floor. That place was a zillion times bigger than the cage at the puppy store. By all means, that house seemed new as fresh paint. It turned out the housewarming ceremony happened the same day they brought me in. You could say I felt super proud and super lucky to be a part of that family.

The moment Dad walked in with me, he loosened his grip, and I instantly leaped upon the floor." Loki leaped onto a patch of sunshine on the grass.

"Whoa!" Luke leaped a little too.

"Blame it either on the house for being too big or me for being too small, I didn't have a spark-in-the-ocean idea of what I was supposed to do at that moment. You live in a cage for as long as you can remember and suddenly find yourself in the middle of the unspeakable wilderness of a big human house. Your thoughts and emotions go haywire for half a moment. In the next half of that moment, they enter a bubble. There's too much visual and auditory info for your tiny brain to process. You push all the excess info inside the bubble. The bubble bursts, and then you start running. So I ran and jumped like a hare that'd just discovered its legs." Loki looked at Pixie, subconsciously estimating his size at the time he first came to the house.

"I guess I can vaguely relate to that feeling," Kiko said with a hint of nostalgia in her voice.

"Yes, second that," Pixie followed up.

"It isn't any prettier if you are on the other side of reality—that is, if you are a human. As I was leaping over a thousand imaginary hurdles, the four humans in the house lost their collective cool. Lakshmi ran away from me and jumped up on a table. Sam ran for me as I ran into a room. Finally, someone agreed to play with me, the play I did. I made Sam run after me through thick and thin as Mom and Dad stood in absolute bewilderment. I wasn't used to so much play, and I got tired in the next couple of minutes. Sam was able to round me up in one room and locked it from the outside. Yeah, he won that historic first round," Loki remembered his first real friendship as if it had happened the previous day.

"Ouch, that must have hurt!" Kiko sneered at Loki. But Loki was in no position to stop.

"I didn't mind losing to my big brother. But what I did mind was a big fat cage assembled just for me the moment he opened the room. You bet I did not want to step into that cage. But Sam and Dad put me in there anyway. The rest of the day had zero adventure and lots of loneliness with just the big iron house and me. It was like the puppy store all over again, only a thousand times cleaner and brighter. But what can a dog do? Tuck your tail and tell time to twill for you!" Loki concluded playfully.

"That's bad! How long did they keep you in there?" Weekday intervened.

"Thank heavens, not very long. Dad gave me something to eat, and I dozed off in a minute. I woke up to the commotion of plenty of humans. Lakshmi and Sam had brought in their friends, the whole lot of them. I opened my eyes, and they were standing right outside. They had made a circle around the cage as if looking at an animal in the zoo. As I saw them around me, my tail was doing something it had never done before. Sam let me out of the cage, and we played on the lawn for a while. Everyone wanted a piece of me. Heck, they treated me like a celebrity." Loki gleamed with pride.

"Wait a second. Shouldn't I be the one walking you through the tenets of celebhood?" Little Pixie had already taken offense irreversibly.

"You want to do that right now, little sister, like really?" Kiko did not like that attitude from Pixie.

"Okay, Loks, you carry on. I just thought it was the right thing for me to pitch in as the resident celeb of the group. But yeah, whatever," Pixie defended her celeb-hood by casting aspersions on the celebrity status of everyone else.

"Everyone played with me and left. I was so exhausted by then. Sam gave me water, and I drank it all. I wasn't able to control my excitement. I needed to go pee, and I looked for a spot. I ran around the house, looking madly for a place. I marked a corner for peeing and life. And, ladies, don't mind me when I say this, but it's thrilling to pee in the open for the first time in life. I wish I could frame that feedback and reciprocation from the ground," Loki went on full-rant mode.

"You said it, brother. I dig that feeling every time," Luke invited Loki for a rant battle.

"As I told you, not everyone likes it. Dad was already angry with Lakshmi. That was a new house after all. But how does a pup know that? Anyway, I never peed or pooped inside the house once I knew how much disharmony it brings among humans," Loki resentfully submitted.

"Ask me, and I lived in a house with three dog siblings. I guess it happens with every first-time dog-owning family. Let's move over that and tell me how you gelled with your new family." Weekday was all for making Loki feel good about his family.

"That's a long one. My parents are conservative vegetarian Hindus who happen to be first-time dog owners. Everyone, except Sam, would wash their hands every time after touching me. I always thought of myself as more than cute, actually crossing over into the handsome zone. I never quite understood why anyone would need to wash their hands. That kind of put me off initially, and I did not know how to respond. After a while, I figured they disliked my jumping around and licking. Essentially, I had to curtail most of my basic dog instincts." Loki sighed. He had lost something valuable to the glare of time.

"I am so glad my girls never asked me to cut down on my celebrityhood." Pixie suddenly became grateful.

"But they quickly realized they were dealing with a dog first and a pet next. I guess the family found out that I was a bit sad and 'un-dogly' in my demeanor. They tried to cheer me up with toys and play. Sometimes I would wag my tail purely out of dog instinct. But the very next moment, I would go back to being grumpy," Weekday said in a heavy voice.

"That doesn't sound very cheerful," Luke remarked.

"It isn't. Sometimes I would get angry and bark aloud in the middle of the night. That would wake everyone up and shake things up a little." Loki hoped that would make him look tough.

"I might have done that a couple of times myself. But how did you learn the human language?" Kiko had been carrying that question in her mind for some time.

"I think understanding another language is never a barrier when two beings resonate with the same frequency of love." Weekday framed Loki's mind on that one.

"Wait, did you guys hear that?" Pixie rose from the grass.

"I think that's Jack locking the rear door. That means it is time to go home. And isn't Jack one of the better humans we have seen around? He never locks the door while we are playing but only before everyone leaves." Weekday loved Jack like he loved most humans he knew.

"We could help Jack one of these days," Loki said innocently.

"How exactly do we do that?" Kiko asked even more innocently.

"I can open a few locks myself." Loki had been itching to flaunt his new skill.

"Bonkers, you don't say that. Anyway, checkout time, guys." Pixie's time to leave had arrived.

"Hell, yes! We'll continue some other day." Loki was still excited.

"Okay, bye, the girls must be waiting for me." Pixie waved farewell to her friends.

"See you on the flip side, guys!" Kiko remarked.

"Bye, all!" Luke patiently waved at everyone else.

* * *

When Loki's family first brought him home, they took their own sweet time with him. In the earliest days, he would stay leashed to a post for most of the day. When Vishnu and Savitri had coffee on the patio, they would bring Loki along to play. They were still apprehensive of letting Loki off the leash. Lakshmi and Sam would join Loki for play when they were at home.

It went on like that for over a month. While Loki was happy to be staying with the family, he always felt there wasn't enough play until one day when Lakshmi finally decided to talk about it.

"Look at him. He stays grumpy most of the day. If he jumps around, it will be more fun both for him and for us," Lakshmi pitched in the idea.

"Okay, what are we talking about, exactly?" Vishnu asked.

"How about we send him for training?" Lakshmi was all bubbly, and so was Loki at the idea of housebreaking.

"Didn't we train him for a week last month? It did nothing." Vishnu was clear in his mind Loki would not benefit from another training. Or maybe he thought no training could school Loki.

"I know, I know. But this a three-week-long boarding program." Lakshmi seemed convinced. "I spoke to this trainer who says she will train him to obey commands and not to bite into wires, plastics, etc. More importantly, he can housebreak," Lakshmi pressed her luck.

As happy as Loki was to hear about stepping out of the cage, he was worried again the moment he heard about boarding for three weeks. But it wasn't going to happen unless all four people in the family supported the plan unanimously. While Vishnu seemed reluctant about the idea of a second training, Sam, Lakshmi, and Savitri seemed to have ganged up in favor.

"Okay, if it's anywhere between $500 and $1000, we can give it a shot," Vishnu said. He added, "And that's a lot, considering there's a good chance it will yield in nothing."

"Mmm, Dad. We are speaking of one of the better trainers from New York," Lakshmi said meekly.

"How much better? Mind translating that into dollars, please?" Vishnu came back. He articulated that cautiously. He was worried about how much to spend, and he did not want to look like a miser either.

"Three. Three grand. It's three grand for three weeks," Lakshmi almost murmured while looking at her mother.

"That is way beyond reason—$3,000 is a lot for a couple of weeks of training," Vishnu tried hard to suppress his shock. "Frankly, that is almost double of one credit of your fees at the college. I don't think we can . . ."

Sam had been listening keenly while all this was going on. He hadn't said a word thus far. "You make a fair point, Dad—$3,000 is a lot for two or three weeks of training. You have to choose between a one-time training fee and recurring repairs and replacement costs on torn sofa and footwear," he said calmly.

Lakshmi had already made up her mind by then. She said, "It's okay if you don't want to pay so much. I'll pay the difference with the money I have saved."

It's one thing for any dad to argue about the price of something with his daughter. But no father is going to accept his daughter paying the difference between the two proposed prices. She ought to pay the full thing or pay nothing. That aside, Vishnu agreed to shell out the entire money. Two days later, Loki's trainer Lucy came to pick up Loki and took him to a plush training facility in Upstate New York.

Time passed in a jiffy for Loki. He happily jumped around the training facility following instructions and playing with other dogs. If someone watched him at the training facility for the first time, they could well assume Loki belonged there. Honestly, it was much more than that. He seemed ecstatic like he wouldn't have left that place for a thousand human homes. Had he forgotten about Sam and the rest of the family altogether? That's beside the point. How was the family feeling without Loki? That was the real deal.

For a couple of days, Vishnu and Savitri were relieved, while Sam and Lakshmi were mostly indifferent. Forty-eight hours flew by, and the first wave of longing set in. It spelled out most strongly when Vishnu and Savitri sat out by the patio.

"Doesn't it feel vacant without Loki?" Savitri asked.

"I was about to ask you, but I pulled back. Yes, it feels vacant and somewhat more silent too," Vishnu said with a mild hint of a smile.

"I wonder what they might be teaching him there." Savitri opened a fresh pack of biscuits.

"I doubt if he's even learning anything. Aren't those Loki's biscuits?" Vishnu pointed at the pack Savitri had just opened.

"Oh! I brought this out of habit, totally forgot he isn't here." Savitri tried hard to act normal.

"Which reminds me, this one is perhaps the last of his cookie packs. Remind me to get a few while I come back from the office before the weekend," Vishnu added plainly.

"Sure, but that might not be necessary this weekend. Loki won't be home until the last week of the month." It was Savitri's turn to serve a gentle reminder.

"Is that now? Why does it feel like the idiot's been away for two weeks when it's just been two days?" Vishnu burst into laughter, and Savitri joined along.

Some great scientists dedicated a significant part of their lives' work to prove time is relative. Loki and his family understood that firsthand during Loki's training. For Loki, three weeks went by like three days. For Vishnu and Savitri, three weeks passed like three months, and for Loki's human siblings, Sam and Lakshmi, it was more like three full years without their baby brother.

By the end of Loki's second week of training, two things were brightly clear: One, in a short time that Loki had spent with humans, the family became as attached to Loki as Loki had to them. Two, everybody saw in Loki what Sam had seen in him on the first day. They just couldn't wait for him to come back. None of them cared whether he learned anything back at the training facility. Lakshmi even talked about a premature exit. Those talks died in their infancy because, love and other emotions notwithstanding, all four of them wanted full value for their money. Breath by breath, Loki's new human family crawled through the last week of Loki's absence in patient expectation of his homecoming.

On the day of Loki's homecoming, his trainer Lucy walked up with him, holding his leash with her right hand. She seemed all bubbled up at the success of her latest assignment. Luckily, it was a Saturday, and all four humans were at home. Sam and Lakshmi were ecstatic to see Loki back home. They barged out through the front door as soon they heard Lucy's van pull up in the driveway.

When Lucy saw Loki's siblings approach, she silently dropped the leash and gently patted Loki on his back, ushering him on to his family.

But Loki did not leap and run. He walked—chin up, back straight, and nimble-footed. He almost looked like the dog version of a boy scout. The training had worked!

While Sam and Lakshmi latched on to Loki, Vishnu watched them play. Shortly, he joined the welcome party along with Savitri. It was evident that the parents were still apprehensive about what Loki had learned at the facility. As first-time dog parents, they did not know what constituted good behavior for a dog. Did they want Loki to be as well-disposed as a human child? Did they want Loki to exhibit discipline like the military dogs they had seen in the movies? Or did they just want him to be a natural dog as long as he did not trouble his human family? Wait, was that even possible?

While Vishnu and Savitri were floating on a dense cloud of thought, Lucy demonstrated Loki's newfound obedience and "human orientation" to Sam and Lakshmi. On the face of it, Loki had learned everything that his parents wanted him to learn. Lakshmi and Sam were thrilled that their baby brother would not cause any more trouble to their parents.

He would sit when asked to sit, walk when they wanted him to walk, run when commanded, and of course, fetch when demanded. Lucy put in a good word about Loki and told them how he outmatched everyone at the training and graduated with distinction.

Loki became the dog that they wanted. He stopped howling at night. Heck, he stopped howling all together! The next day the family decided to housebreak Loki. Nobody was going anywhere. Everyone wanted to see how Loki would go about his day without the leash.

Loki knew his game from thereon. That was the moment he had been preparing for the facility. He knew all about the kind of conduct that would set him free from the cage for life. He would have all the house to himself. All he had to do was follow whatever Lucy had taught him. He did just that. The cage and leash became a distant memory for him at home ever since.

Loki was a changed dog after he'd come back from the training facility. The family slowly got used to their new child and sibling. Moreover, the untouchability stopped too. They stopped washing their hands after touching Loki. By all means, it seemed like the next phase in Loki's life with his family. If anybody had shown Loki this picture of a life with family at the puppy store, he would have said yes in a heartbeat.

Loki considered himself lucky to have a loving family, like so many other dogs. He would often look at Sam from a distance and be lost in vacuum amid a thousand oddities. He would still feel just as warmly for Lakshmi, Vishnu, and Savitri. He would lovingly goof around the lawn when the family was there and chase an odd butterfly or two. But something had changed. Deep down, something did not add up. He felt happy; it wasn't that he did not. But that happiness did not feel complete.

Something strange was holding Loki back from being the adamantly happy pup around the family. He could not decide whether it was the fear of being caged up all over again or losing whatever little proximity he had managed to stitch with the family. Or was it something entirely different? After a while, the family also took notice.

There was a glaring discrepancy between the light in Loki's eyes whenever he saw someone come near him and the coldness with which he would greet them. Sam was the first to realize. He understood better than anyone else how Loki wasn't acting like the kid he was and how his little brain was always processing what he should and shouldn't do.

It jagged Sam's memory. He had seen this happen to another child, a child he knew. On odd days, he would look long and hard into the mirror, trying to find a living memory of that child. There were only so many of those memories as snowflakes in hell. It went back to a time when he lived in a cage. But you could see the cage only with Loki. For Sam, it had taken him a while to realize the "whats" and "hows" and "whys" of his invisible cage. He knew the damage too well. He knew he couldn't throw Loki under the same bus. Sam found his opportunity when the family gathered for coffee the next day.

"Look at him play. I don't remember seeing him this happy like forever." Lakshmi was more smiles than words.

"Hasn't he been the good boy in the last few weeks?" Savitri resonated with Lakshmi word to word.

"I'd like to think so," Vishnu said, the skepticism in his voice hardly going unnoticed.

"Think so? Anything wrong, Dad?" Lakshmi came back sharply.

"It's nothing, just this thing about yesterday evening. I saw Loki zoning out by the living area. I was going to bed and asked him to come with me to sleep in the bed."

"You invited Loki to sleep in the bed." Sam was intrigued.

"Yes, I did," Vishnu said.

"Wow, I can't believe that, Dad!" Lakshmi was doubly bubbly.

"But the dog wouldn't budge," Vishnu added with a tone of regret.

"Holy me! I thought he'd be thrilled. Lakshmi couldn't add up.

"I didn't even know you asked him to sleep on the bed." Savitri hated being in the dark, especially about things happening inside her house.

"He has drawn the line." Sam put in grimly.

"Wait. What? What do you mean by 'drawn the line'?" Savitri was unimpressed.

"Nothing, I just mean he might not have been in the right spirit last evening." Sam dodged the first round of shelling.

"No, you did not mean that, *anna* (brother)." Lakshmi knew Sam was on to something.

"Drawn the line? Those words are too heavy to mean nothing. What gives, son?" Vishnu walked across and placed his hands gently on Sam's shoulders.

"Let's not talk about it, Dad. You and Mom may not like what I say." Sam dropped his shoulders.

"Chin up, son. Say what you have to," Savitri egged him on.

"Sorry, if this comes across as rude, but how can you possibly be so blindsided? You are doing the same thing to him that you did to me years back," Sam blabbered meekly.

"Whoa! I am going to give you guys some space." Lakshmi figured nothing else to say. She silently got up and started walking out.

"No, no. You can stay. This conversation is as important for you as it is for Mom and Dad," Sam urged Lakshmi to stay.

"Okay, I'll stay if that's what you need." Lakshmi nodded in approval.

Sam continued, "There is always a time and place for discipline, and I want you to know that I am not against that. But force-feeding discipline to a child by keeping him away from friends and simple kid stuff like sleepovers, how fair is that?" Sam was more startled than everyone else at the sudden rise in his pitch. "When Loki first came to us, all three of you would wash your hands each time you interacted with him. He was so little he couldn't tell his nose from his elbow. But I guess he was big enough to feel that he belonged in the lawn and not in the house."

"Oh, Sam. My boy! We never meant for him to feel that way." Savitri was both moved and alarmed.

"And I am sure you never meant to make me feel the same way while playing the hardball discipline game with me all through my childhood and, in fact, until very recently. You see, Mom and Dad, we can only control what we say and do to people. We never know how that makes them feel." Sam paused briefly.

"Don't stop. Go on. I want to hear the full thing." Vishnu dragged his chair right in front of Sam.

"Honestly, I don't want to stretch this, Dad. But loving a child is not enough. You must also let them breathe. We all know what's more important in life between love and breath." Sam was sweating and fuming in equal parts.

"That, and I also read something about dogs having their body discipline and how it can be contradictory to human training," Lakshmi added enthusiastically.

"It's deeper than that. I wish I could give you a glimpse into what I felt. Most of my friends grew up like normal children, while I formed up like a never-ending lab experiment among all of them. Of course, with lots of love involved. I can never, in my right mind, fault you for not loving me enough. You loved too much, way too much. So much that it felt like custody." A warm tear rolled down Sam's cheek as he shuddered under his breath.

"Ah, my boy! My little boy. I am so sorry." Savitri rushed to Sam, hugging him tightly.

"All we have ever wanted is the best for you, Sam. Never did we realize that we hurt you so much in the process. But I can tell you this: If you forgive us now, you will feel lighter than ever," Vishnu said as he gathered around the huddle.

"I have zero context of where *anna* is coming from on this one. But I am lucky as hell that you covered so much for me since we were little. Nevertheless, let me squeeze in too. We haven't had a family hug in ages." Lakshmi joined the party.

As the family juggled between bitterness, nostalgia, and newfound warmth, Loki stood there alone, all by himself. He had long stopped playing as he was patiently listening to the family roundtable. And long conversations, especially passive ones, make a dog hungry.

"Can we break for some food and be back at it again?" Loki interrupted what a growing and lengthening-by-the-second family moment.

"Oh, you come here, big boy." Lakshmi dragged Loki into the big family huddle. For a moment, there was zero sound around the house. Only was an inevitable and strange lull. The calmness, the silence—they were all making a statement—a family had found togetherness all over again. Loki, a dog that barely remembered the smell of his mother and siblings, brought a massive change in the family. Lakshmi realized how much Sam meant for her because she wouldn't have to endure the things that Sam had been through already.

Right there, at that moment, Loki helped fill up a large, invisible crack within what seemed like a happily involved family. After that, while Loki seldom climbed up the bed on Vishnu's beckoning, he was definitely at greater ease with the family than ever before. Sam finally started speaking to his parents about the small stuff in his life.

CHAPTER 3

The Backyard Bout

One cloudless night, he cast his fishing net high into the sky.

Some stories write themselves. For some others, you need a husky inside your house. Add a visit from a chance raccoon to your backyard. Now bake that up with an orthodox Hindu vegetarian family, and you have the full platter. Well, almost. The F5 would often ask Loki if he had ever eaten meat. Just in case someone isn't up to speed with this, Loki didn't know the taste of meat until he was three years old. Yes, for the first two years of his life, a husky living—bang—in the middle of America was brought up on vegetarian food.

Also, this Siberian Husky might never come across steak in his life. Why? Those living under a rock are generally the ones to not know how precious the cow is to a Hindu family.

Loki would often say this to his F5 friends: "I'll never have beef. The cow is sacred to my parents, and they'll never do it. How many times do I need to tell you guys?"

This particular incident happened a year back. Loki was growing fast, even faster inside his head. That was the time when he just couldn't wrap his mind around this new topic that they had been discussing at daycare. Hunting was all over the place. Every dog, small or big, F5 or not, could not find a more prominent subject to talk about. Some of that talk looked like it was straight out of elementary school.

"Don't you guys carpet me with that collective smeared grin again! I proudly stand by what I said," Pixie declared valiantly.

"Yes, Chihuahuas fight duels with smaller mammals down in Mexico. And the Spartans fought the Persians in the Battle of Thermopylae on Miami Beach." Luke fired the opening shot.

"Stop pulling her leg. One, it's oh-so tiny. And two, I did Google the thing about Chihuahuas hunting in Mexico. Seems legit, they do it quite regularly." Kiko took Pixie's side, albeit after considerable teasing.

"Yes, and I hear they are pretty accurate too," Loki pitched in. Until then, he had heard the others patiently.

"No, no, no. You guys don't even believe what you are saying. All you care about is how small or big or gnarly or gory a dog looks. Can't you just be blind for once? And maybe use your imagination for a change?" Pixie vehemently protested.

"I hear you, Pix. I have often wondered. What would it look like if all of us had to hunt for our food? Just like our ancestors did?" Weekday lent excellent support to the tiniest dog in the gang.

"Yeah! The wolves do it all the time. Why can't we do it?" Pixie tried hard to evoke emotions in others.

"I guess we can. The real question is why we won't do it. Just this morning, I was walking with Dad around the park. And there was a squirrel, running right past me. I am more than sure she challenged me for a race." Loki found a reason to buy Pixie's story. Hell, he just figured it was his story she had been narrating.

"Ohh, what? Did you race it?" Luke fumed at Loki.

"Of course not. Dad wouldn't let me. I wanted to give that ant of a squirrel a run for its life. But Dad held on to the leash as hard as he could. Had I tugged at it any harder, he would have fallen. So I let that thing squeak past me. Dad realized how disappointed I was and, for the hundredth odd time, showed me that darned park sign, 'All pets must be on a leash,'" Loki answered, overcoming his discomfort.

"How do you know it was for a race? No squirrel in their right mind and body outruns a husky." Kiko was bemused at the audacity of the squirrel.

"You bet. The animals think we are their pals, partners in a frickin' relay race of some kind." Now Weekday saw some meaning in the story.

"That is what I am getting at. These small-timers look at us as some kind of equals. They have no fear of us. They have no respect for the food chain, damn it!" Loki was clear in his head.

"Twitch! I can't be the only one that's mildly startled at the sound of this," Kiko inserted playfully.

"Wow, the food chain? I never looked at it that way." Pixie followed Weekday in trying to poke a little bit of humor.

"But now that I do, it sounds catastrophic. Is the world ending in a week or what? Who will Loki run with or, pardon me, race within the park?" Kiko swung a mud ball at Loki.

"Wanna laugh? Go ahead. But one day I'll break the wheel of this human-centric synthetic ecosystem that has denied us natural evolution." Loki was determined to do something about that.

"But what are you going to do, champ? Break off the leash and chase a squirrel? I am sorry, I meant race a squirrel. Oh, I am terrible at framing these things." Pixie saw an opportunity, and she jumped in.

"Totally with Pixo on that one. Ahem, I am majorly sure she implied no violence. Or did she, Mr. Killing Machine Ultimatrix?" Luke taunted Loki.

"Joke about it all you want, losers. But I promise you this: The next time you guys see me, there'll be blood on my hands. I mean it." Loki wasn't enjoying that conversation, and he made everyone know that.

"Behold, ye lesser dogs walking planet earth! There goes Loki—the god of mischief and the annihilator of smuggler-squirrels at the joggers' park. Popcorns must sell at double their rate the moment Loki walks past." Luke fought Loki at all planes.

"Give him a minute, guys. You don't know just when to stop, do you?" Weekday couldn't just watch everyone blow up on Loki like that.

"I don't give a squirrel's tail to what these losers think. All I care about is the food chain and my place in it. And if that means blood, blood." Loki sounded dead serious.

"Okay, this is the place where I ask you to stop getting ahead of yourself and respect the law." Weekday was worried about Loki.

"Law made by humans to govern humans," Loki scoffed. "Do you know anything that this law of yours mentions about the *Food Chain*? Yes, I said that—'Food Chain,' with a big F and a big C. The type of food that is 'Uncooked' and requires 'Killing,' again, big U and big K." Loki sounded grim.

"Don't know about the law making a mention of the food chain. But I am sure everyone in the food chain needs rest at some point in time. As I see it, you need rest just about now." Weekday tried to douse the flames of the conversation.

"Wow! That escalated quicker than Kim Kardashian's luck!" Kiko couldn't let on any rest to her soul.

"Hell, we need to break this. How about I tell you guys about Zen and an incident that happened at college a while back?" Pixie saw a possible way out of the unpleasantness.

"As in your homie's ex-flame? And is it about the police thingy that happened there lately?" Kiko looked at Pixie.

"Yes, that one. And the story is about the story behind the police thingy. You guys in or not?" Pixie confirmed.

"I am in this. Right about now, anything that does not involve blood, killing, and the Food Chain, with a big F and big C, will do me just fine." Weekday cast the first vote in Pixie's favor.

"So this one time, Hannah, Zen, and I went to the vet's, and then Zen secretly smuggled me to their college," Pixie recollected.

"Wow. Wait. Didn't your college have that rule about cat-sized pets at their college?" Something wasn't adding up for Luke.

"Yeah. That changed a while back—also, a lot of other things. Now, story or not? You guys tell me." Pixie decided to up the ante.

*   *   *

No, Loki did not stop thinking about the food chain even after a long, tedious, and seemingly cooked-up story about a Chihuahua helping the police grab hold of a bunch of illegal weapons inside a college campus. Even several hours of rest did not help. It was one of those rare occasions that he decided Weekday's advice wasn't worth it. And something inside him seemed to be boiling. He felt this urge he had never felt before.

Loki knew this was coming. Why wouldn't he? He had been battling this for a long time inside him. For the first few days, he thought he would get away with it unharmed and the urge would subside in time. But sometimes there's this demon inside you that grows bigger even as you fight it. The harder you fight, the bigger it gets. But was this fight even necessary? Why couldn't Loki do just what his biology asked of him?

When Loki puts his heart and soul to something, an opportunity presents itself sooner than later, only this time the opportunity disguised itself as a full-grown raccoon on a warm afternoon. Sam and Savitri were at lunch. They'd generally leave the backyard unlocked so Loki could step out if he wanted.

That afternoon Loki wasn't feeling particularly well. He was lying down, his mind still vaguely caught in the ever-expanding labyrinth of emotions and urges. He heard something hustle in the backyard. *Must be the silly wind again*, Loki thought. Even his mind was making noises now. Some more hustling followed! It didn't look that windy a day when Loki was at the park with Dad in the morning.

There had been news of burglars in the neighborhood. But no one would ever dare enter a house with a husky in it. Nevertheless, Loki had to know what was going on. So he decided to step out, pacing himself with mixed caution and aggression. My word! What did he just see?

It was a raccoon—a big furry raccoon! Loki paused briefly. The raccoon had Loki's cereal bowl. Loki had never seen this creature in the backyard. So he just kept looking for some more time. Why was the raccoon there? What was he trying to do? Why, rather, how dare he touch Loki's bowl? And most importantly, what was his rank on the Food Chain? There was only one way to know.

"Hey, what are you doing here?" Loki asked the raccoon sternly.

The raccoon had no idea he was under observation. Like Loki had never seen him, he hadn't seen any of Loki either. The shock was mutual. For starters, the raccoon seemed to have no idea whether Loki belonged to the house or was just a simultaneous visitor.

"Who are you?" the raccoon threw back, doing his best to sound confident.

"You answer first. And what are you doing with my cereal bowl?" Loki was quick to sense the shakiness in the raccoon's voice, just like the raccoon was quick to understand who belonged and who didn't.

"I just came here to play, like I do every afternoon with my friends." The raccoon was quick to act healthy.

"Which friends? Don't you know this is private property?" Loki fumed.

"Oh, I didn't know. Nikki, Vinni, Tony, and I always thought this was a park," the raccoon said with a slight grin.

"Hold on. Have you been here before?" Loki was clueless.

"Yes, we play here every day in the afternoon. I have never seen you around though. Are you a friend of the family, or have you come here to play too? In case you've come to play, I must say you've made a forgettable first impression, mate." The raccoon made it evident he was smart.

"Shut it. I am not here to play. And I am not a friend of the family. I am the family." Loki was furious at the "outsider" implication.

"Oh, so you are the baby boy that they keep jailed in the house when we come to play in the afternoon? I am so sorry to wake you up." That jibe instantly mailed a chill down Loki's spine.

Did his parents know these guys came to the backyard in the afternoons? If so, why would they keep him locked?

"Watch your tongue, intruder. No one's jailed here." Loki pretended he didn't feel the insult.

"Arlington! Thou holy angel of raccoons! I am so scared right now. What are you going to do, baby boy? Chase me like the squirrel you race in the park?" The raccoon sling-shotted that out of nowhere.

"What did you just say? Say that again, your furry ball of nothingness." Loki swallowed his shock and turned it into a cannonball of fury in half a millisecond.

"Sure, sir. Will you chase me like the squirrel that you never got to chase in the joggers' park because your daddy wouldn't let you off the leash. There, I repeated it. Let me know if that suffices or Your Majesty would need something more elaborate." It was evident the furball was enjoying it.

"What? How?" Loki couldn't wrap his head around that.

"Hahaha! You, sir, are a subject of common admiration in the raccoon community. Baby raccoons around the neighborhood go to sleep with tales of your valor." Another sharp jibe, just like that.

"Stop right there. Or I'll tear that tongue from inside your mouth. I kid you not." The dog sounded mean.

A sensible lesser mammal would have taken the warning for what it was, especially if that came from a senior in the Food Chain hierarchy. But this friend of Nikki, Vinni, and Tony didn't realize he was about to cross a line he wished he hadn't.

"Or what, baby boy? Will you kill me? Erase my existence? Leave me bleeding at midnight and howl at the moon? Summon the angel of death? Go ahead, do it. Your daycare mates still wouldn't believe you did it." The raccoon laughed hysterically at his own delivery.

That last bit about the F5 set Loki off. He felt as if his mind was in the middle of a million hell fires. He paced back a couple of steps as genetic coding took over his being. With one swift flight, Loki landed his paw on the raccoon's temple, almost instantly knocking him unconscious. He grabbed the thing by this throat, internally rupturing his jugular vein. By the next minute or so, the raccoon had stopped breathing, and its heart had stopped beating. Loki killed it without spilling a drop of blood.

The experience was as exhilarating as it was satisfying. Loki held his head high with the trophy between his teeth. Then he did a little parade of a walk around the perimeter of the backyard.

It was time for Loki to taste the kill and feel blood on his teeth for the first time. Loki was about to tear into the raw flesh of the raccoon. Just then, his mother and brother came running and screaming, almost as if they'd heard a gunshot. Well, they had heard a gunshot, just that the gun was inside their living room all the while. Sam and Savitri couldn't believe their vegetarian dog had robbed another being of its life.

He had proven a point, neither to his parents nor to his siblings. It wasn't even to his mates at the daycare but to himself. Loki could hunt! He felt incredibly proud and utterly drained.

"Let that thing go, Loki!" Sam yelled.

Loki seemed adamant. He wouldn't let go. His mother and brother darted at him and tried to remove the raccoon from between his jaws physically. The two of them made such commotion that a couple of neighbors came rushing for help. It was quite a scene as Loki started running around the backyard with the raccoon and the humans began running after him. If the audio on was muted on all this, it might have even been funny.

After a while, Loki was so exasperated that he couldn't run anymore. He let the raccoon out of his mouth. Sam got hold of him, finally. Loki was panting as if he had swum across the Atlantic. It was not because of tiredness. He would often run with Luke and Kiko for hours at a go and never break a sweat. Some days they would just keep running until one of the F5 parents picked them up and dropped them at their respective houses. But that was new. Loki had never felt such exhaustion. Maybe it was sheer nervousness or maybe because he had broken a rule of the house.

"Blood! He is bleeding. The thing bit Loki!" Savitri screamed her lungs out.

"Don't panic, I'll call an ambulance," Sam huffed pantingly.

"Call your father first." Savitri tried to gather her breath back.

When Sam called Vishnu and informed him of what had just happened, Vishnu was happily shocked. Yes, the father was happy about Loki retaining his instincts despite his vegetarian upbringing. Sam couldn't believe his ears. He put the phone on speaker.

"Did you just say 'very good'? Are you out of your mind? Come home right now. He's bleeding. That thing bit him, come and get him to the hospital!" Savitri yelled at Vishnu.

The funny thing about humans is this: No one might ever know how much they love you and care for you unless you are hurt. Loki was hurt. And Savitri was raising hell. It was then that Loki realized that Sam's mother was his mother too. He always knew that in his heart. But the way Savitri yelled at Vishnu for not responding with alacrity, that was Loki's moment of truth.

Sam, Savitri, Lakshmi, and Vishnu were trotting dozens of sixes and sevens. They rushed Loki to the nearest emergency and forgot the rest of the world even existed.

Three hours in the emergency made Loki feel he was a reborn saint as if an angel had cleared his mind of all negative thoughts. The antibiotic and anti-rabies shots had knocked him out flat. When he opened his eyes, he saw the F5 all around him.

*   *   *

"Ah, guys! I feel weightless. What day is it?" Loki threw the faintest of smiles at his mates.

"Same day, Mr. Killing Machine Ultimatrix registered blood on his hands," Kiko said with a smile that looked more like a statement of remorse.

"I am sorry, guys. I think I got carried away," Loki said regretfully.

"Nothing to be sorry about, Loks. That son of a racitch must have tried to get under your skin," Pixie tried to cheer Loki up.

"Yeah, how did you know about it?" Loki still couldn't wrap his head around just how much information the raccoon had about him.

"Well, Pixo did some digging. It turns out the raccoons around the town are pretty well informed about things," Weekday said in a massive, concerned tone.

"And we have a mole in the daycare. The fellow's been leaking info about us to the raccoons. Their plan goes deeper than you would imagine," Luke stepped in.

"But you don't worry about all that, big boy. We'll get to the bottom of this. You just focus on getting back on your feet," Pixie reassured Loki.

"I can see a war coming," Weekday said in his classic grim tone.

"Is he up? Is he up?" Savitri hushed into the room. "My boy, my little boy, never do that again."

The sainthood did not last very long. The F5 spent most of the winter in one another's houses as everything, including the daycare, remained shut under the snow. A new year arrived, the snow melted, and spring came by. Spring seemed somewhat tricky at first. For starters, Loki missed the snow, and he missed the snow too much. Nothing in this world seemed as inviting as snow.

Spring brought freshness. Everything seemed green. As much as Loki loved the winter, he'd happily concede that he had seen an awful lot of snow in the past months.

The first bit of green that Loki could latch on to was right in the backyard. For Loki, playing in the green grass was not as exhilarating as dashing in the snow. But it was fun, nonetheless. As Loki took a liking for playing around the lawn, his afternoons would pass happily. On most afternoons, some of his other mates from the F5 would drop by.

One particular morning, it was warmer than usual. Loki was playing alone in the backyard. Kiko was supposed to join him, but she was running from her morning training. Loki was chasing the odd butterfly and whatnot. Right then, a birdling came circling down and nosedived right before Loki in the backyard. Thankfully, there was enough grass in the garden to make for a soft landing. And boy! Loki was curious or what. He had never seen a bird from such proximity.

The birdling tried to move as Loki watched curiously. It was helpless, barely even able to get back on its feet. Loki felt clueless. He thought the little thing needed water. So he tried to pick up the bird inside his mouth and carry it to one of his water bowls in the backyard. What happened next was unreal. The birdling sent out a distress signal as soon as Loki tried to pick her up. The message was so loud that Loki was summarily startled. He leaped backward in surprise.

Within seconds of the distress signal, some thirty-odd grown-up finches swarmed the backyard. A dozen of them surrounded the birdling from all corners. Loki watched in bewilderment as the rest of the birds started toward him. There were so many of them, and they rushed at him noisily. Before Loki's mind could wrap around the angry birds and how to deal with them, the birds started pecking at him from all corners. They were literally all over him.

Loki was playful as the first few birds came near him. He jumped in excitement and swirled all around the place. He was pretty sure they were coming to play with him. Next, two or three birds pecked on him. By the time Loki sensed the danger, all the other birds had come to fight him. Outnumbered and out of his wits, Loki called for the attention of his parents.

"What did I even do?" Loki barked at them.

The angry finches didn't take any of it. They kept pecking at Loki's body as if he were the one to blame for the little bird. Loki wasn't finding it funny anymore. He wasn't feeling the brunt of the beaks, thanks to his thick coat. But he was irritated at so many birds poking at him, some even at uncomfortable places. So he did the gentlemanly thing by giving a couple of soft warnings.

The warnings did not amount to much either. The birds came down even harder at Loki. He was feeling the beaks on his inner skin this time. For the first time, Loki felt the pain. But he knew he couldn't hit back at the finches. Mother had forbidden him from hurting anyone post the raccoon episode. He wasn't going to disobey her just because some pesky flights were acting above their pay grades.

But Loki had had enough. All he had tried to do was help a small bird get some water. What he received in return was a full-scale assault from a tribe and a half. So he did the second best thing at that time. He curbed his instinct to retaliate and let the elders at the house know there were intruders in the backyard. He barked so loudly that it scared both the birds and his parents inside. The birds backed off immediately.

Savitri, Lakshmi, and Vishnu came running for Loki. They managed to shoo the birds off the backyard.

"Why would they even want to hurt him?" Lakshmi shouted.

"Are you hurt, my boy?" Savitri was ransacking Loki's coat for signs of injury. There were none.

"Thank goodness, there's no injury to him, those things were snaring him for nothing." Lakshmi was just as bewildered at the birds as Loki himself.

"Why didn't you hit back, son?" Vishnu quipped. Everyone was bewildered in their own ways. Loki looked at Vishnu, and then he looked at Savitri. That was his way of cutting a long story short.

"Why would you even say that? Weren't you all there when I had asked him not to hurt anything anymore after that thing bit him?" Savitri snapped back sharply at Vishnu.

"I don't understand this nonviolence business. Are we raising a husky or a teddy bear?" Vishnu fired as coolly as he could.

"Oh, you, men! And your thirst for blood. Would you stop watching those overrated anti-physics action flicks of yours already?" Lakshmi would never miss an opportunity to get under her dad's skin.

"Stop it, you two. Let's get Loki back in. It's time for his breakfast anyway." Savitri was hastily still searching through Loki's coat.

"Oki, Loki momma. Come on in, big boy. I'll get you double breakfast since our big brother ain't home either," Lakshmi said with a slight grin as her parents went back in.

Loki was not ready to leave yet. He did not even budge. He sat upright, his head still. Generally, when Loki would sit like that, Lakshmi knew it meant he was heartbroken about something.

"What's the matter, Loks? Are you not hungry yet?" Lakshmi couldn't decide what had gone wrong. She went near him and sat down on the ground. "Come one, you can tell me. Don't we have our tiny secrets, li'l brother? I am sure we could add one more to the bank," Lakshmi said, softly caressing Loki's forehead as she spoke.

Loki did not say much. He just laid his chin on Lakshmi's lap and whimpered softly. *What could have gone wrong with him?* Lakshmi thought to herself. Loki was the type of guy that's always ready for his breakfast on time. But then breakfast was calling, and Loki did not want to move!

"Are you hurt, baby brother? Do you want to come to the vet with me?" Lakshmi's voice dampened at the sight of her ever-energetic baby brother feeling so low. Loki still did not say a word. He exhaled slowly and sunk his head deeper into his sister's lap. "No? Yes, I am not much of a fan of your vet either. It's nothing much, just that I am generally allergic to people who prioritize injections over pills at any stage in their lives." Lakshmi made another veiled attempt to cheer him up.

Loki stayed put. Then he got up and shook himself lightly. As Lakshmi was still at sixes and sevens, trying to make meaning out of what was happening, Loki limped across the yard and trotted in circles near a point around the corner. Then he sank again.

"Mom. Dad." Lakshmi's voice almost choked at sight. "Do you guys mind coming out for a second?" she freakishly shouted at the top of her pitch the moment she saw what was going on.

Vishnu and Savitri stormed back out to find Loki almost broken down, and Lakshmi was weeping as they'd never seen her cry.

"Dear, dear lord!" Savitri's mouth uttered without her knowing.

It was the birdling. It was still there, lying around the corner, barely breathing, by all estimates, breathing its last. And Loki was broken out of the disappointment of not being able to save its life. His parents might have wasted precious time arguing over huskies and teddy bears—time they could have used to save a little dying bird.

Savitri knew better. As a medical professional herself, her gut knew there was still some time. Or was it just her emotions backing up Loki's?

"Rush, rush. Get some water." Savitri shook Vishnu's arm violently.

"Get up, girl. Save your tears for later. Run back in and find the car keys," Savitri said to Lakshmi, gently messing up her hair.

"And you, Mr. Undertaker. Are you coming to your favorite vet with us or not?" Savitri said to Loki in a tone with equal parts of sternness and love.

*   *   *

That morning Loki learned three things: One, no one loses hope over life when a doctor is around. Two, when a dog goes out of his way to save a small birdling, he makes a friend for life— the kind of friend that keeps coming back to you, no matter whether Kiko finishes her training on time or runs late. Three, there will be challenging situations in life. But more often than not, Mom's got it covered. Savitri's touch of care, her unconditional love and a semicomatose break from reality, pushed Loki into another dimension of reality, one that was the same cute shade of gray as Loki. That reality was furry and big enough for Loki to roll in and hide inside without you even noticing.

CHAPTER 4

A Resolute Resolution

The greatest loss is when you lose the bliss of ignorance.

You don't quite comprehend the relativity of time unless you have a pack of awesome friends living it with you. Weeks swish by in days, and what feels like an arduously tiring day for the working class glides like a few buttery minutes on a hot pan. The F5 was living life like time had stopped for them. It was the very zenith of their friendship. They felt like a picnic of five small kids floating atop the time-space gridlock inside a giant bubble wafted by their imaginations, blissfully unaware of the struggles and realities of their very existence.

Unfortunately, bliss borne out of ignorance is often due for a reality check. The funny thing about reality is it checks you when you are least ready for it. It could be through unpleasant stuff like abuse, violence, accident, death, or seemingly pleasant manifestations like new friendships, long conversations, and even new people in the family.

Loki and his friends would often have long conversations about maximizing their friendship through a well-planned and meaningfully-long adventure trip. The frequency of these conversations grew increasingly thicker as their friendship grew denser.

"I really thought we were good friends. But you guys know you can't fault me for seriously doubting that now." Kiko raised an eyebrow, which implied a sudden alarm. She'd mastered and polished this unique technique of drawing attention over some time.

"What? Why would you say something so terminal? You know the F5 is just recovering from the horrors of World War 2," Pixie protested. Actually, after a point in every conversation, whatever she'd say would either be a protest or a complaint.

"Yeah, not funny." Kiko made a face.

"Then what is? Pray, tell us, your Kikesty," Pixie complimented her with another.

"I didn't mean it that way," Kiko clarified.

"We are listening." Luke switched off his listen-only mode.

"All I am asking is, what kind of friends do not go out on an adventure?" Kiko blew through the bubbles.

"We go out on so many adventures, don't we, Weekday?" Loki showed some interest too.

"There you go, exactly my point! I am talking about adventures that, one, don't wrap up in sixty minutes or less and, two, Weekday wouldn't approve of for a change. Also, weddings do not qualify as adventures, irrespective of how many pounds of carrot cake we demolished at Sam and Lisa's wedding," Kiko said while trying hard to put on a furious face. But she could still not hide her smile at the mention of the carrot cake.

"Ahoy, Alice in Wonderland! Not for nothing, but how many times are we going to go over the same thing again and again? Can't we just plan something this evening and be up and moving in the morning? And yes, I beg to differ about your hypothesis of carrot cakes not qualifying as a genuine adventure," Pixie said gingerly. She was many things, but un-spontaneous wasn't one of them.

"For starters, if you guys think you can ruffle my feathers by calling me an old dude, good luck with that. I couldn't care less." Weekday went stage one into developing that characteristic grin of his.

"We totally understand, Weekday. Please don't feel we are devoid of empathy. Everyone is somewhat careless at your age. You never have to explain that, at least not to us." Kiko hit hard and, had it not been for Weekday, hard enough to win a cage fight, argumentatively speaking.

"Come on now! Weeko has sea legs when dealing with all these. We get nothing out of him, not even a grin. Okay, maybe just a grin." Loki was ever so quick to jump to Weekday's defense. But even he couldn't resist the temptation to train a wild shot at Weekday's somberness.

"But what about our big adventure? Weekday never approves of any of our plans. I am all sick and tired of the other daycare dogs bragging about their adventures. They aren't half as cool like us, and those morons are going places!" Luke tried to anchor the conversation back to where it started, and someone had to.

"Only last week, Spark and team came back from the West," Kiko articulated the obvious. Everyone had been thinking about it until that point, but none of the F5 had made mention, maybe slant and suggestive inklings, but never a real mention.

"Right, they went with their parents. From all that we have been circling in the previous discussions, none of you is willing to speak to your humans about this big-ticket adventure of ours." Weekday tried to diffuse the melancholy in the news, nicely aware that it wouldn't suffice.

"I don't endorse rashness for a second. But what is the point of an adventure if humans surround us and leash us all the time we step out?" Luke told the others exactly why he thought Weekday's argument wasn't enough.

"Can't beat that point with all I have, Weeko." Even Loki couldn't defend Weekday for that.

"Yeah, I see. You guys crave inviting danger that it's difficult to talk sense into you." Weekday spoke his mind.

"Like every time, this is a pointless discussion. We are better off chasing butterflies at one another's homes for the rest of our lives. The world can wait until we are reborn as snakes." Luke was done going around in circles over the same subject for the five-hundredth time.

"Or whales. I would love to be reborn as a big fat blue whale. I might even become the first mortal whale to travel all seven seas," Pixie added her bit on large animals.

"What's an unreal whale? And since we have touched the subject, make me Thor next time around. Both the hammers, please," Loki said that, no surprises there.

"'Til then, let Spark and other lesser dogs have all the fun. With or without humans, who cares?" Luke had given up.

"Speaking of Spark, I haven't seen the guy in a while." Kiko brought some curiosity back to the conversation.

"I was just about to say that myself. It's been almost over a week since I saw the small dog. Spark can't stop poking his nose around our area whenever he is at daycare." Pixie somehow seemed to enjoy calling dogs younger than herself "small."

"Hate to break this to you guys, but Luke and I have picked up some rather unpleasant chatter about Spark." Loki accorded more attention to the topic. A wave of moderate inquisitiveness mailed through the others.

"Is it? Pixie and I heard a few weird things from the girls the other day. And they can't stop giggling about it. Bitches." Kiko faintly recalled a few things she might have heard the other day.

"You have to stop using that word in that context. How many times do I need to tell you now?" Pixie took a stand.

"Hold it, am I missing something here? Where is Spark? What happened to him?" Weekday was either at sea about Spark or was just playing along.

"Umm. Ahem. It's the N-word, Weekday," Luke said, with more suggestion than fact in his tone.

"What? Spark got nuked?" Weekday said, genuinely surprised. He clearly wasn't playing along.

"You bet, Weeko. There have been rumors of all kinds about it," Loki said disquietly.

"Was he also told they were taking him to the fluffy toy store?" Luke started to sail close to the wind.

"Or was it the usual 'we are going to bring your baby brother' bit?" Kiko knew how things worked in the male-dog territory. She'd rarely had female friends.

"I am betting on the 'cute girlfriend.' Every guy-dog falls for it. Every time." Pixie knew things too.

"Haha. We sure do. I was told the same thing too. What did your humans tell you, Weekday?" Loki admitted and quickly realized Weekday was somewhat unforthcoming on the subject.

"Yeah, tell us. You must remember every bit of it," Kiko insisted, partly because she always liked pulling Weekday's leg.

"Ah, I remember the day like it happened yesterday. I was playing fetch with Sylvia, John, and Superdog. Ginger and Cherry had gone out with Henry to a nearby town to attend some lectures. I still wonder why Henry always took those two with him and not any of us." Weekday drifted along nostalgically.

"Aww, I can imagine you were playing with your siblings, Weeko, like little hurried furballs bouncing up and down around that grassy backyard. But I think I know why Hank always took Ginger and Cherry only. I guess he preferred the ones that loved a little bit of adventure over young dudes who give up on fun and turn to ascetic uncle-ism early in life." Kiko seemed to have enough fuel to keep charging at Weekday all day. It was evident she saw Weekday as the first obstacle to the adventure she so severely craved.

"Wow! You never run out of the mud to sling at Weekday, do you?" Luke said, evidently a tad disturbed at the unidirectional onslaught.

"I am sorry, I was kidding. I know Weekday doesn't mind. Unless, of course, the rest of you add enough fuel to it." Kiko almost realized she'd stretched a bit too far but wasn't willing to give up just then.

"Oh, I never mind. Plus, there's truth to what Kiko says. We boys were totally into playing indoors while Ginger and Cherry were mad about hitting the road, backpacking, long drives, and all that. They would chase Henry all through the weekends just to hop into the van and drive away to nowhere." Weekday drifted more into nostalgia as he went past the banter. His mind had this strange setting that allowed him to tap into distant and pleasant things whenever he wanted to escape the chaos around him.

"That puzzles me somewhat. Does Weekday ever get along with weekends?" Pixie tapped into her turn to mock the furry dog.

"That's unfunny, purely because of the number of times you guys said it yesterday." Weekday gave one back.

"Yeah, my bad. What's purely funny is how you cannot stick to the root conversation and stray all the time." Little Pixo got carried away with Kiko's apparent success at winning banter battles with Weekday.

"Yeah, I thought you would follow up with something as unfunny. Did I ever tell you guys that bullying people older than you is still bullying?" Weekday played a classic card.

"So are you going to cry now?" Kiko was quick to capitalize on that turn in the conversation.

"No, I just won't tell you guys about the root conversation and all the branches associated with it. I am sure we can live with that." Weekday summarily dismantled the opposition, sweetly hinting that they'd been playing into his game all the while.

"Why, Weeko? Aren't you supposed to be our unconditional guardian angel? That is so unfair." Pixie threw the reconciliation trope the moment she realized the furry dog had had the better of her.

"As I am reconsidering it at this moment, that does sound a bit unfair. An apology seems fair to me though. What do you guys think? It always helps to have a mixed bag of opinions." Weekday blew the last nail off the coffin, showing everyone how dead and naked the debate was.

It had been a while since Weekday had been trying to teach his fellow dogs the importance of choosing the right battles. Fighting alone doesn't make you a hero. "You first ought to choose the right battles," he'd tell them so often. But the mind asks for proof and demonstration. So Weekday would often demonstrate the principle in such conversations.

"Okay, you win. I am sorry. Now go ahead and tell us what happened to you, John, and Superdog?" Kiko waved the white flag.

"That's more like it," Weekday acknowledged her surrender, momentarily abandoning his deep state of nostalgia. Then he thought aloud.

Despite some classic narration, the story Weekday told about the neutering of his male siblings and himself did not inspire any courage in his friends. Frankly, it depressed them. What it brought about was a rekindling of thoughts and conversations that none of their parents would want to hear.

"What strikes me hard is how we always found this topic merely enterprising enough to laugh about and never really had a serious discussion about this." Loki took a long breath; he had almost forgotten to breathe while listening to Weekday.

"I know none of you like hearing it. But I think I am a little depressed right now." Luke could not hold back.

"Can we please talk about something a little more pleasant? How about watching a movie at my place this weekend? The girls said they wouldn't mind the house full of dogs every weekend." Pixie was quick to realize the gang was sliding into mass depression. She ran a few paces around everyone, trying to break the thickness of the air around their corner of the daycare.

"Sounds like an idea to me—that is, if we can look past the inherent speciesism of it." Kiko lifted a dead twig off the grass and sifted through it.

"Sure, I am in. Love me some movie-watching any old day of the week. But as usual, I get to choose which movie." Weekday pretended he was all cheered up.

"I wish I could join. But Sam and Lisa are coming home this weekend. I haven't seen them in months. Like every time, Mom and Dad have invited the whole neighborhood for dinner. By all means, you guys continue. Count me in if something comes up next weekend," Loki said like he was somewhere in the middle of excitement and remorse.

"In a parallel universe, dogs would choose other dogs over humans for their weekend plans," Luke said out of nowhere.

"Really? Like are we really going there again? How many times do I need to tell you how important my family is to me and how much these conversations upset me?" Loki protested instantly. Every time Luke said something like that, Loki would wonder if that was the last time and if Luke would stop shooting such stinging arrows at him and the others.

"Yes, the family is important. All of us know that. But what about V? Wasn't she important? Did you not promise yourself you will go find her? Or have you forgotten all about her now that you have a cushy life and a big car? Tell us, Loki, do you even love her? Did you ever love her?" Luke abruptly paused as if something had hit him, most probably the realization of what he had just done.

* * *

During his initial days in the fighting pit, Luke had developed uncanny ways to sting both with his blows and his tongue. Each word he said stung Loki more than a million finches pecking at him. Loki felt weightless. A strange high-pitch noise was filling his ears. He couldn't hear his daycare mates speak anymore; it was just their lips that moved. Almost everyone was saying something to Luke. But Loki couldn't listen to them. It was like he had lost control over all his senses.

Luke had never said something so sharp and caustic, at least not to Loki. But Loki knew something more significant. He knew that it wasn't

Luke that hurt him. Ever Since Loki shared his puppy store experience with his daycare mates the F5 had never spoken about V.

Every conversation about her had just two participants: Loki and his heart. Yes, Luke wasn't the first guy to ask him those questions. It was a somewhat routine conversation that Loki had with himself every night, every night right till the point he could console his heart to find some sleep.

What truly hurt Loki was the ruptured boundaries of that conversation. He felt violated in a strangely painful manner. And honestly, it was more shame than hurt. He was ashamed to give his mates the same excuses he was so used to giving himself every night. And was there even an excuse? Perhaps there wasn't. The truth was Loki had fostered deep and inalienable attachment with his human family and their smiles. Maybe what he wanted for himself did not matter anymore.

Yes, finding sleep was still tricky. Every time Loki closed his eyes, V's face showed up like magic on a conjurer's canvas. Her little whiskers, her upright ears, her moist nose, her big eyes, and the glow in them every time he called out her name. None of that was imaginary. He had seen it all for real. Loki could live with that image in his heart for the rest of his life.

Loki circled through thoughts about how his mother would think of V, whether she'd like V or not, how would the siblings get along with V. He would answer himself with justifications like "What's home after all? Isn't it supposed to be the place where kids stay with their moms and dads, their biological mothers and fathers?"

The more Loki thought about this home, the more radically his thoughts veered toward his mom—her touch, her furs, and the warmth in them. Of that was followed by those dreams about his mom, dreams that were soon shaping up like nightmares.

As the rest of the F5 kept rebuking Luke for what he said to Loki, the latter was staring blankly, messy congestion of profound thoughts shrouding his mind. But Loki was shaken, not broken. He quickly realized he did not want to be part of a conversation where someone judged his love for V. Luckily, Loki sensed Vishnu's car pull up outside. He shook himself gently, gathered strength from all his body, and stood up on his feet. As he was about to exit through the door, he thought he heard Luke fumble some meek words of apology. Loki did not mind; he kept walking.

While driving back home from daycare, Loki seemed a tad cold to Vishnu. Generally, he would sit upright and look out of the car when Vishnu drove him back home. On odd days, he would even whine about

Vishnu, not letting him drive. Not that day, not that drive. The more he thought about those lines from Luke, the deeper he slid into the messy dungeon of abysmal thoughts.

That night Loki kept twisting in his bed as he could not sleep 'til late in the night. He just could not get over what Luke had said. The more he tried to think of different thoughts, the more his mind would pander to his most deep-rooted fears about his mom.

It was the same nocturnal routine, only that night he felt more ashamed, more guilty. The overwhelming cyclone of zigzag emotions had spiraled out of his control. An involuntary whimper followed. It came straight out of his heart. Loki had run out of excuses to pacify it.

He went back to his toy basket and brought his favorite childhood toy, hoping to have a meaningful conversation with it. Even that did not help. So he did something that he hadn't done since his training at the New York facility—he howled. It was a long wet howl with a searing sound of pain rising out from deep within his belly.

Loki sat up and howled for as long as his lungs would let him. Then he shrunk back to his space, snuggling his nose inside his tail. For a moment, he just wanted to vanish and stay that way for the indefinite future. There had been multiple such moments throughout that day, the first coming right after Luke had dropped that truth bomb. Alas! Reality is the worst enemy of hope.

Moments later, Savitri came rushing. "What happened, dear? Is everything okay?" she asked Loki, gently placing her palm on his forehead.

"Yeah, I am ..." Loki tried hard to say something legible without looking at her.

"Can you please put him to sleep? I had a field day at work, and there's a big client meeting tomorrow," Vishnu said from the inside.

"Sleep now, big boy. Daddy has a lot of important work tomorrow. I'll drop you to the daycare in the morning." Savitri caressed Loki some more, placed his head on her lap, and hummed a mellow lullaby. She knew she couldn't leave Loki all by himself on a difficult night.

So Savitri sat right there on the rug, gently gliding her fingers through Loki's furs. She folded his ears backward and rubbed them slowly, using only so much pressure as to shape a cotton ball. Everyone in the family knew how much Loki loved that and, more importantly, how quickly he dozed off whenever someone did that to him.

"Go back in, Mom. I am sleepy now," Loki said as he heard Savitri yawn. But she sat there long after Loki had fallen asleep.

When Loki woke up the next morning, Savitri was still by his side, and his head was still on her lap. She hadn't slept the whole night. She hadn't slept the entire night because her baby boy had trouble sleeping. And that, right there, was Loki's biggest dilemma. This family was showering that kind of abundant selfless love on him that it was practically impossible for Loki to explain it to his friends.

The developing love story between Loki and his human family was begetting a thick, intensifying conflict within himself. A chunk of that happened without him even realizing. Was he giving up on his dog family? Would he be able to keep the promise he had made to V? Would he ever be able to see his mom and play with his siblings again? Would he ever be able to tell Vishnu, Savitri, and his human siblings that he wishes to see his dog family?

If anything, what Luke had said acted as a catalyst to this intensifying conflict in more ways than one. Effectively, Luke had forced him into an impending conversation with himself. He had been indefinitely procrastinating for ages.

"Mom, did you not sleep? Were you there the whole night?" Loki gently nudged Savitri's hand, his head wriggling inside her lap.

"Yes, yes, I slept. And no, I came just a while back to check on you. Haha! Look at me. I must have zoned out on top of you." Savitri was bluffing. She wanted Loki to feel that she took no trouble for him.

"Mom. We had a deal. You don't lie to me. I know you didn't move an inch from here. That's how I could sleep so well. I feel like I have woken up after a year." Loki fitted words inside a long yawn.

"I just could not leave you like that. Now you tell me. What made you so depressed?" Savitri could add comfort to her voice just like that.

"Nothing much. It's just been so long that I have seen Sam and Lakshmi. I miss them so badly." That was the best Loki could devise at that moment. All that was going on with him aside, Loki did miss Sam, Lisa, and Lakshmi.

"Oh! Is that all? Wait with me for just another couple of days, dear. Sam and Lisa are coming home this weekend. You can play with them all you want. But you don't make Lisa run behind you," Savitri said.

"Why? What happened to Lisa? Is she not well? And how long will it take for Lakshmi to remember she has a baby brother called Loki?" Loki's eyes gleamed of childish fury.

"Oh, nothing happened to Lisa. It's just that she feels a little heavy in the belly these days. You'll find out more about that when they come. And I'll let Lakshmi know how you feel. She'll also be here soon." Savitri tapped Loki on his forehead. Loki always seemed to ask her more questions than she could answer.

"Okay, I won't play hop and run with her. Will you please go to bed now? You haven't slept the whole night. I'll ask Dad to drop me at Weekday's place when he leaves. Henry will drop us to the daycare." Loki wanted to speak to Weekday before anyone else at the daycare.

"You gotta be quick if that's the plan. I leave in fifteen minutes.," Vishnu was right behind them, eavesdropping on some classic mother-son conversation.

"Okay, Dad. I'm ready. I'll have breakfast with Weekday." Loki stood up and wiggled whatever residual sleep was in him.

"Before you go, boy, tell me if you are inviting over Kiko to meet Sam and Lisa this weekend?" Savitri knew just the line to fire Loki up.

"Mom! Why? Why do you have to do that when Dad's around? I have told you Kiko and I are just friends. And no, no one's coming over here on the weekend. They are heading over to Pixie's to watch a movie." Loki stared more than he said.

"Oh, that's like a super plan. You should join your friends too, right?" Savitri was in no mood to sleep before she pulled enough of her son's leg.

"No. I am staying back home this weekend. A guy I call my brother and the lady he calls his wife are coming over after a long time. So you see, I have to reject your kind offer," Loki jeered.

As Loki jumped into the car with Vishnu, he knew it wouldn't be an easy day at the daycare. As sorry as Luke would be, everyone else would still bash him plenty. Or would they?

"Hey! I forgot to ask. Were you under the weather yesterday?" Vishnu broke the ice.

"No. No, Dad. I guess it just wasn't windy enough yesterday. You know how much I love the wind on my face," Loki responded even before Vishnu had completed as if he had been contemplating the answer. He and Vishnu hadn't had a proper conversation in weeks. It was mostly because of Vishnu's tight work schedules, but Loki hadn't made any real advances either.

"Oh, I thought someone from the daycare might have told you something bitter." That was a somewhat routine line Vishnu used to hit deploy against Loki.

"No, no. No. Not at all. Why would anyone tell me anything?" Loki gave it away with the haste.

"I see. And you want to meet Weekday before you see the others at daycare?" Vishnu asked gravely. He knew something didn't sit right with Loki.

"By the way, why didn't you wake me for the walk today?" Loki amused himself. It took him so long to discover that they had skipped the park that morning. That was the first time Loki and Vishnu didn't go to the park in the morning while both of them were at home.

"Ah! About that. I came to you in the morning, as usual. You and your mom were sleeping like babies. Your mom wasn't even lying down properly. You were snoring so loud I thought you might need some extra sleep," Vishnu said with equal happiness and amusement. He was happy that at least for a day, Loki did not tornado him out of his sleep.

"I thought as much, Dad. You wanna step out and say hi to Weekday before you leave for office?" Loki asked Vishnu as they pulled over outside Weekday's house. The man was happy. Loki had found some great friends at the daycare.

"I'd love to. But I am afraid I am awfully late already. Be a good boy and tell Weekday and the others I sent love." Vishnu seemed in a real hurry.

"Have a good day, Dad!" Loki said as Vishnu and Weekday waved at each other.

"And lest I forget, your mother might not be able to pick you up from the daycare. She said she needs to do some shopping for Lisa. So, you hang out at daycare for an extra hour or so, and I'll be right there," Vishnu said and sped away.

"Gosh, Weeko! Last night was a curse from hell. Without Mom, I might have never gotten any sleep. Do you have some breakfast handy?" Loki told Weekday as they stepped inside the house.

"Yes, breakfast. You've been on my mind, Loki. I called you back so many times while you were stepping out. We all did, as you were leaving the daycare. You did not even look back." Weekday sounded earnest.

"I guess my senses blacked out, and I couldn't even hear you guys. I just felt I should leave the place, and that's what I did," Loki submitted.

"Umm. Maybe you did the right thing." Weekday backed him up.

"Is Luke all right? I thought he might be feeling low." Loki voiced himself softly.

"You thought. The boy was reeling under criminal guilt. We had to console him for longer than we bashed him." Weekday pushed his point.

"I feared as much. What do you think I should tell Luke?" Loki felt confused and sad.

"Tell him that you are all right that you have forgiven him. He thinks he's messed up your head." It was more appeal than advice from Weekday.

"He thinks? He messed up my head, all right!" Loki fumed.

"Yeah, he did. He did. I didn't mean to undermine the impact of what he said. Here, your favorite bowl of cereal," Weekday said as he passed Loki a bowl.

"I don't know what he was thinking. But what he said was just not done." Deep inside Loki could still not believe Luke had said something like that.

"I agree, it was wrong. But sometimes, Loki, we have to judge people by their intentions and not by their words. You know Luke has had a rough past." Weekday pressed his palm softly onto Loki's.

"Yes, yes. People are products of their pasts. You've told me before." Loki was still visibly irritated.

"And now is the time to act on it, little brother," Weekday pressed harder.

"I know. Okay, I got carried away. But I could barely sleep even with Mom beside me all night." Loki sounded low.

"Was it that dream again?" Weekday was inquisitive.

"I wish we could still call it a dream. It's getting worse, more nightmarish every night." Loki had real horror in his voice even as he was chewing upon his favorite breakfast.

"Oh! I am sorry. How bad is it?" Weekday inquired.

"How bad, you ask? What's the deadliest horror movie you have ever seen?" Loki looked up at Weekday like he meant it like he wasn't fooling around.

"Umm, I am divided between *Silence of the Lambs* and *The Shining*," Weekday inferred after a few seconds of thought.

"Neat. Now imagine being forced to watch those movies every night against your will. No, I framed that wrong. Imagine you went to sleep with good thoughts, got hijacked in your sleep, and were sucked into those movies, of course, all involuntarily. And it doesn't end there. They swapped the victims and placed you instead, just where the victim was. There's more—you can't escape the cyclicity of this horror because you can't escape the necessity of sleep. So even if you don't want to experience any of it, you give consent, just by going to sleep. That's exactly how it feels." Loki was rendering at the top of his voice by the time he had finished.

That allusion Loki gave Weekday shook the earth beneath the latter's paws. One, Weekday couldn't quite comprehend the magnitude of the horror that Loki must have been through. Then it was one of those rare occasions when Weekday did not know how to respond. Thankfully, Henry came along and broke the ice, calling on the two of them to join him in the car.

While Weekday, Loki, and Henry were driving to the daycare, Loki's mind went back to the conversation about Weekday and his brothers getting neutered. Most dogs don't even get to know what happens to them until they realize they are an organ short. But Weekday was too smart not to know.

And yet Weekday did not protest. Neither did his brothers. How could they give up on their desires so easily? What were they thinking? Did they know what it meant for their generations to come? Instead, the ones that would never!

Loki was staring fondly at Weekday as Weekday was gazing blankly through the woods. *Even for a collie, Weekday looked way older than his age,* Loki thought to himself. No one could ever know what must have been going between those thick brows. Weekday had lived a better life than most dogs on the planet. And yet his countenance bore the semblance of a sad picture seated deep inside his heart, sadness reminiscent of a life that could have been. It was melancholy gestating out of an inherent preference toward a more compassionate version of reality.

Then Loki stumbled upon a strange realization—Weekday had thought about these earlier. The graveness in his voice, the heaviness in his demeanor, everything contributed to this singular reality. The reality was Weekday's mind was all too consumed with self-conversation about the same questions that Loki had only recently conceived in his mind.

That was Weekday. Then there was the broader issue of cutting through the conversational divide with humans. Every dog in the history of human-dog companionship had nothing but love for their humans, the magnitude of which has ever so often outgrown love for their kind.

To their parents and every dog parent ever, the F5 and all other dogs were and would always remain cuddly little kids devoid of any adult thought and emotion. Who, if anyone ever, would bell the proverbial cat?

The car drove in resonance with the commotion of Loki's thoughts and continued right to the point where Loki and Weekday bumped into Luke at the entrance of the daycare. Soft words of apology and acceptance followed, and the trio slowly walked in.

"Oh! So you two have made up, I see. Too bad, I had some extra popcorn for round 2," said the smallest dog in the room as she winked at Kiko in acknowledgment of the success of their little plan of stationing Luke right at the entrance of the daycare.

"Yeah, we know better than fighting over the dead and buried. We are dogs, not vampires," Luke said.

"Hard to believe a former fighting pit champion does not consider himself a full-blown vampire," Kiko remarked with a grin.

"No, I object. We are not dredging that up, at least not now." Pixie put her little foot down on the matter.

"Yes, please. We've had enough bad blood in the last twenty-four hours," Weekday gently weighed in.

"My bad! Apologies to the whole cast and crew of F5," Kiko submitted immediately. She realized she had stepped into forbidden territory.

"Hey, it's all right. The pit wasn't as bad as in the movies." Luke looked the other way, clearly uncomfortable at the very mention of the pit.

Luke had left the fighting pit for good. That happened a long while back. All that he could remember about the hole were distant memories of hungry dogs with survival in their eyes and death on their claws; that, and the wild cheering from the blood-thirsty dog entertainment enthusiasts in the gallery.

But the fighting pit had never left Luke. Even the smallest mention of the hole would spark a dreadful whirlwind of memories, all leading up to the labyrinth of self-sustaining and largely irreversible trauma. All the fights he had fought, all the blows he had landed and fielded, just about everything reeled by his mind, as if a juggler had racked everything up in his deck and flashed all fifty-two cards between Luke's ears within a split second.

"Seven," Loki shot through the brief quiescence.

"What was that?" Kiko asked.

"Seven, I said seven," Loki reiterated.

"Yes. Three. We heard that three times. What about that?" Pixie snapped like that every time something confused her.

"Seven cats and dogs are born for every new human in this country," Loki said and looked straight into everyone's riddled eyes.

"Wow! That's some serious leverage. If this is a plot against the human establishment, please be advised that it's ethically impossible for me to work alongside cats. Anything else, I am on board." Pixie was amused and somewhat even excited.

"I am in, with or without dogs. Let this cruelty end once and for all." Kiko took a sweeping jibe at the universe.

"This is serious, guys." Loki cut Kiko in between.

"What's it that you see and we don't?" Weekday asked.

"We would be seven times the population of humans in this country alone. That's the reason they neuter and spay puppies and kittens. There'll be far too many of us, apparently." Loki sounded too serious to entertain any insensitive blabbering.

"Oh! I see. You haven't gotten over it though. This neutering and spaying topic makes me feel so giddy." Kiko was the first to react.

"Slam your ears shut for a moment, Kiko. I am interested. So what is it really, Loks? Are we and those little beasts seven times of the human population or not?" Pixie's interest in interspecies warfare was abnormally high.

"Also, can we just walk out to the play area for a moment? It feels nauseating around this corner." Kiko was evidently still giddy.

As the F5 walked out and into the play area, Kiko and Loki paused for a moment to check on Luke. The latter hadn't spoken a word ever since the mention of the fighting pit. He had just been staring at his claws, vaguely absorbing what everyone else had been saying. Shortly after, they joined the others in the play area.

"This isn't about warring with other earthlings, Pixo. And no, we are not 2.1 billion in this country for heaven's sake. That is what we would have been without neutering and spaying, much more because dogs and cats reproduce more frequently than humans. The math is complicated, you know." The F5 gravitated toward Loki, making a small circle around him as he spoke.

"All right. So humans neuter and spay us because they don't want us to be more than them," Luke said after listening carefully to the others for a while.

"Yes, in parts. But I don't think it is limited to who has more numbers, humans or pets. They see it as a larger problem," Weekday added.

"What's the larger problem?" Kiko was curious.

"The larger problem isn't 'why.' It's 'who.' Who will look after so many dogs and cats?" Loki revealed his bit.

"Umm, now that I look at it, seems like a legit concern to me," Pixie said persuasively.

"Wait, we shall decide on the legitimacy and validity of it later, once we hear all sides of the story," Luke jumped in.

"Yes, all sides. Literally. How do they do it in other parts of the world?" Pixie traded the attack mode for a more well-informed stance.

"Sorry to break your heart, guys, but I am afraid your plans for global conquest will have to wait another day. We are ten minutes past closing time now." That was Jamie, the stand-in daycare keeper.

"By the power bestowed in me by the holy trinity of rain, mud, and earthworms, I forbid all members of the F5 to think of any other thought before we reassemble at this very spot," Kiko said jubilantly.

"I am coming in an hour early tomorrow. Who else is on board?" Pixie sprung on top of the late evening grass.

"Everyone! Breakfast at my place at seven." Loki assumed collective responsibility like always.

Twenty hours went by as the F5 hardly batted an eyelid. Similar thoughts occupied everybody's minds. Humans have the United Human Rights Commission to fight against atrocities inflicted on humans. What do dogs have? In addition to all the love, care, and affection, human children are born with human rights by default. What about dogs? No one in the F5 had ever heard of dog rights. All they'd heard of was this vague and instead umbrella notion of animal rights.

The thought of animal rights could have been interesting to the F5. But how many animals did they know? Do all animals have a common standard of living and a common purpose in life? Does a cow want the same set of rights as a turtle? And how on earth could you club dogs and cats under the same set of regulations? The mere thought of it was revolting to Pixie.

The F5 honored Loki's breakfast invitation the next day. Homemade munchies vanished faster than a UFO's blip on the earth's radar. Twenty minutes later, they regrouped at their favorite spot at the daycare.

"Tell us about it. How is the global dog community going about this imposed celibacy business? But before that, are we so dependent on humans that they think we are all finished without them? When did a dog not know how to take care of herself between the vast blue sky and the cool, wet earth?" Kiko said, quickly realizing during the breakfast earlier that others had put in more research than her.

In all honesty, that was the neatest trick of the morning. Whenever you are low on research, feign some good old inquisitiveness. The guys that do put in the study appreciate genuine inquisitiveness in seekers.

"I wish it was so simple. I wish there were a black-and-white division of this. No one is right, and no one is completely wrong here. Different places seem to have different prejudices about us animals." Weekday rose out of his breakfast-induced thought-slumber.

"That's what I read too," said a befuddled Pixie.

"Humans themselves have different opinions on this. Some activists are against neutering and spaying all together," Weekday said with a smile.

"Oh, they are our friends then!" Pixie exclaimed.

"Yes, they are. But each of us has been spayed or neutered because our families voted in favor. Are our families, not our friends then?" Loki remarked, his words reverberating through an eerie silence that cut through the room as the rest of the dogs wrapped their heads around it.

"Yeah. It's complicated. Then there's a different set of activists who believe an unchecked population of dogs will end up causing accidents on the roads," Luke said.

"Of the ones that are picked from the roads and put into shelters, many are put to sleep, like forever." Loki dropped another truth bomb.

"Then there's the commercial aspect. Neutering and spaying is a big business now. So trust our vets to keep inventing new benefits to cajole our humans." Weekday hammered the final nail on the coffin.

"This stuff is messed up. Shouldn't we have a right to choose whether we want it or not?" someone added.

"I guess that is what it boils down to—asking for consent," Pixie submitted meekly.

Spanning back the last twenty-four hours, the F5 had looked at the issue from some perspectives and did a fair amount of research on it as well. But they never thought of that one word—*consent*. It just never occurred to them. When an occurrence becomes too common to ignore, it becomes a part of a tradition. And every so often, a culture so easily overrides values like consent and independent thought.

"Bonkers! They look at us like perpetual babies. Like they do not ask children whether they need vaccinations, they do not ask us whether we seek to raise families when we grow up." Kiko veritably debunked the consent myth. "I guess the thought doesn't even cross their minds. It keeps happening because it's been happening for so long," Kiko added.

"Argh! I wish I were born a giraffe in Africa or maybe even a rattlesnake!" Pixie leaped as high as she could, giving off a near-accurate estimation of her height if she were a giraffe.

"I sometimes wish I were a giraffe too. But here in America! No one should have to give up on the carrot cake we get here," Luke added quickly.

"That reminds me, how are dogs and cats treated in other parts of the world, Weeko?" Kiko asked.

"Not as badly as wild animals, to be honest. No one around the world hunts us down, you see. Unless you are the crap out of luck and happen to pop the bubble bang in the middle of China," Weekday said with his characteristic grin.

"But humans keep killing and eating other animals, don't they?" Luke asked.

"Yes, they'd eat anything that isn't poisonous and, more importantly, isn't cute," Weekday said, actually more "smeared" than "said."

"Oh! Right! How could we forget? It is 'cuteness' that saves us then. Only if half of humanity found the cow cute, there would be no steak." Loki ground his teeth.

"Or let's say they did eat us. We'd at least get to spend time with our families before we ended on their plates. I say the cows got the better deal!" Kiko sneered.

"Holy cow!" Spark broke into the room. "What are you guys even talking about?" he quickly added.

"Umm, nothing, nothing! Just building a quick list of the best steak joints around town." Kiko leaped to answer before everyone else.

"Oh! Yeah! Oh! I thought as much when I heard steak. Do any of you folks have some handy?" Spark swallowed a lump of his saliva.

"Umm, no. Sorry to disappoint you, Sparky. We do not eat steak when Loki is around. None of us eat steak anyway." Kiko was always the first to be triggered by Spark's presence around the F5.

"Oh! No. Yes. I mean definitely. Loki is here, here is Loki. Why would you guys even think about steak?" Spark drew a small imaginary circle and paced a few quick rounds around it.

"I'll be on my way. Monty must be waiting for me in the Small Dogs Circle," Spark spurted out of the F5 stronghold.

"Am I the only one that's thinking this, or has this guy lost it ever since he was neutered?" Kiko gave voice to just about everyone's thoughts.

"To be honest, I always found him weird. Every cat-face dog is weird by default. But yes, Sparky's been an exceptional weird since they took away his family jewels." Pixie broke into little laughter halfway through her quip.

"That reminds me, Sam and Lisa are coming home tomorrow. I better be on my way home now. I need to go shopping with Mom. Weeko, you mind giving me a lift with Henry?" Loki hurried outside to check if he could see Henry's car out.

"Yeah, sure," Weekday said.

"Look for Hannah too, Loki," Pixie went running behind.

Luke and Kiko packed up shortly after Weekday, Pixie, and Loki, leaving in between what was shaping up to be a meaningful conversation until the point Spark arrived. What they did not realize was they were so engrossed with the talks, it was nearly closing time at the daycare. Over the last few days, that had been somewhat routine for the F5. At one point, none of them ever wanted to come to the daycare how times had changed.

"You remember, Luke? There was a point where you and I couldn't stand within the breathing space of each other," Kiko hushed at Luke as they waited for their humans.

"Oh! Yes, I do. We were all so sour back then. Nobody took any real liking to the daycare. Those were the days—fun, play, ignorance," Luke recounted while gazing at a spot in the pathway.

"Ignorance was such bliss, still is for those who have it." Kiko looked into the pathway as well.

"Yes, bliss," Luke said meekly.

"Hey! I am sorry I mentioned the pit earlier today." Kiko had meant to apologize to Luke all day.

"That's all right. Maybe I deserved it for what I said to Loki the other day." Luke still sounded like a meek version of himself.

"No one deserves to be hurt," Kiko said as her car approached.

"Only if that was up to us to decide. See you tomorrow." Luke waved to Kiko as she stepped into her car.

*   *   *

Later that evening, Savitri and Loki did enough shopping to settle a small neighborhood on an undiscovered Pacific Island. Ever since Loki had come back from his three-week stint at the New York facility, he had become her go-to shopping partner. Loki enjoyed it too. Looking at and sniffing around new stuff in the store thrilled him. The idea that he could look at them every day by bringing them home thrilled him even more. But that shopping spree was somewhat different. Loki was too much of a grown-up for some of the things Savitri was adding to the cart.

"Mom," Loki nudged Savitri.

"Yes, tell me," Savitri responded.

"Am I missing something here?" Loki quipped.

"Missing what, my boy?" Savitri replied as she turned a pack upside down for its label.

"Umm, I don't know. But I stopped playing with soft toys like twenty-five years back. Mickey Mouse! Like really? Who plays with Mickey Mouse anymore? Can we at least do an Ironman, please?" Loki pleaded. There was so much meaning in his voice, Savitri froze for a moment.

"Oh that. Don't mind that, we have a big surprise for you in a couple of weeks," Savitri said joyously.

"Then whose is this? Is there a new baby in the neighborhood? I don't remember hearing anything about it," Loki wondered.

"How do you know it is a new baby and not a new pup? Quickly, roll me the cart. We missed it in the last aisle." Savitri seemed both curious and excited.

"Do I even need to answer? Wouldn't you ask me for an opinion if it was a pup?" Loki pulled a long face.

"Oh. How could I be so dumb? You get me all the time. Don't you, Loks?" Savitri tossed a few more items into the cart.

"If you say so. At the moment, I just hope you do not forget Sam's favorite cookies in the middle of all the kid stuff," Loki said with a grinning smile.

"You are such a sweetheart, Loki. I almost forgot about that." Savitri looked at Loki with a full-width smile.

"Mom, what is Sam going to bring for me? Do you have an idea?" Loki could not hold that thought in himself any longer.

"Must be something special. But I don't know about it. If I knew, you'd know too." Savitri did not look at Loki.

"Mom, I have told you before. Never lie to me. I overheard you speaking to Sam last evening. You asked him to bring something for me." Loki summoned his long face contours again.

"Ah, you can't mind that, Loks. I keep asking him what he's getting for each of us every time he comes home." Once again, Savitri faced away from Loki while she spoke.

"Yeah, but you never ask for me. It's okay if Sam forgets to get something this one time. He must be having so many things on his mind. And I am not a kid anymore." Loki turned to the side Savitri was looking and placed his paw on her palm. That was his way of conveying that he understood that there was no need for an explanation.

"I did not think so much about it, Loki. I just like the look in your eyes when Sam brings things for you." Savitri tried to end the discussion.

"That look discovers itself only when Sam brings me things by himself. I guess sometimes we just need to agree that priorities change for people. It hurts less that way." Loki wasn't ready to let go of the fact that Sam had barely spoken to him since the last time the two of them saw each other.

"Okay, Loki. Okay. That's okay. You know and understand so much that it is difficult for me to have a conversation with you sometimes. What do you guys keep talking about at the daycare?" Savitri could not have replied with more excellent honesty.

That was not the first conversation between Loki and Savitri that ended on a note of disagreement. The mother-son duo had had several such small-scale bursts in the past few weeks. Savitri was essentially reliving her days when Sam used to be an adolescent teenager, and they disagreed on just about anything under the sun. *Like that stage had passed with Sam growing older, it would be over with Loki as well,* Savitri thought to herself. Anyway, she had other things to think of before Sam and Lisa came home.

Loki himself hadn't given much thought to the frequent disagreements with Savitri, the thinning conversations with Vishnu, and the total lack of interaction with his human siblings. But all those were pinching at him whenever he was by himself. If anything, these people mattered to him, more than he ever thought they would. But why did he care anymore that evening? Soon it would be night. Another bout of the cyclical nightmare would follow. Then morning would come, and with the morning, his brother from another mother. It would be a happy day.

"Loki, boy! Ready for the long weekend walk?" Vishnu woke Loki up in the morning as had slowly become usual.

"Ready, Dad." Loki wiped his face with his paws.

"Only this weekend, it won't be as long." Vishnu tickled Loki.

"Why? Oh, am I late again?" Loki could hardly open his eyes.

"No, you are right on time. Your brother and his wife are coming home today. Don't you remember?" Vishnu asked.

"Yes, Sam and Lisa. Yes. How could I forget? What time are they coming today, Dad? And when's Lakshmi coming home?" Loki was as excited as he was sleepy.

"You are coming to the airport with us, or would you rather be with your daycare friends? Don't worry about Lakshmi. She'd be here in a day or two," Vishnu teasingly told Loki.

"I thought I would go to the airport with you two. But since you have mentioned, I will drop by at the daycare and greet my mates while we go to the airport." Loki knew how to get back.

"As you like it, son," Vishnu agreed.

*   *   *

As Loki waved past the F5 while leaving the daycare for the airport, his memory swiftly jogged back to the day Sam first saw him in the puppy store. Loki closed his eyes. Those eyes flashed again before him—jet-black, full of life, and so full of love. No part of the life Loki had been living until then would have been possible if he hadn't fallen upon those eyes if those eyes hadn't befallen upon him.

So much had changed between Loki and Sam in the last three years. Sam graduated from college, took a job 2,500 miles away, and married the woman he loved. But to Loki, Sam was still just those that pair of jet-black eyes that chanced upon his little existence and toppled life as he knew it. If

Loki had a home, it was because Sam shared his home with him. If Loki had a family, it was because Sam shared his family with him. If Loki had a father and a mother, it was because Sam brought him home as his brother.

Yet the two of them hadn't spoken for the last month. Loki would remember Sam every day. The truth was Sam also remembered Loki just as frequently. The little pup he picked up from the store had gone on to become the pole star of the family. As Sam stepped toward the arrivals, clenching his wife's left hand. Loki was on his mind too. Did he have to be reminded to pick a gift for Loki? How could he forget?

Sam and Lisa zoomed out of the gate. Sam saw his family from a distance. Savitri and Vishnu were frantically looking at their watches and phones. Loki was looking at Sam. Sam saw Loki and paused for a while. Loki's head was ever so tilted, just the way he used to look at Sam from a distance. Lisa jerked Sam's hand and waved to Vishnu and Savitri, signaling him to move on. But wait, Lisa used to be so lean. Why did she put on so much weight? Loki was baffled.

"Come on, Loki, come on. They're here, they're here," Vishnu asked Loki to join as Savitri had already sprinted to Sam and Lisa.

Loki did not sprint. He walked a slow pace toward the couple and gently sat between the two of them. There was a certain sense of calm that Loki would always experience when he was near Sam. Sam touched his parents' feet. Lisa leaned forward too. But Savitri immediately took her in her arms, insisting Lisa should not lean forward in her condition.

"Can you please leave the walkway?" Someone in the airport politely told the family they were preventing others from passing through the gate.

Minutes later, the family was in their car, driving back home.

"Liz!" Savitri said softly. "Have you thought of a name yet?" Savitri gently placed her hand on Lisa's belly.

"No, Mom. I am so stressed out every time I come close to a name," Lisa said as she rested her head on Savitri's shoulder in the back seat.

Wait, who were they naming? Why did Lisa look so exhausted? What was it that everyone in the car knew, and Loki didn't? Then it struck Loki. Lisa had the olfactory signals of two individuals in her. She was with a child. How could Loki not notice? His brother was about to become a father. He was about to become an uncle. And something inside Loki told him it was about to happen very soon. A sudden gush of adrenaline happiness took over Loki.

"Mom, Mom, Mom," Loki gushed like a baby fountain. "Can we please speak for a second?" He pushed Savitri to a corner the moment they stepped out of the car.

"Yes, yes. Help Lisa to her room, will you please? We will talk right after." Loki sprung to Lisa's help as she had considerable difficulty getting down from the car, almost pushing Sam from her side in the process. His excitement knew no bounds.

"Slow, Loks," Lisa said softly, holding her bulge with her right hand. "Here, come to my left," she added, brushing his back gently.

Minutes later, Loki stormed into Savitri's room.

"Why did you not tell me?" Loki demanded.

"Tell you what, Loki?" Savitri said with a teasing tone.

"Sam and Lisa are having a baby!" Loki said his words in what was a hushed, low-intensity scream.

"I wanted to surprise you, Loki!" Savitri said with a smile.

"I am surprised, surprised!" Loki made a quick tour of the room. "Is there anything else around this place that I do not know about?" Loki peeked below the bed and inside the drawers.

"Now don't be jealous, go ask Lisa if she needs anything," Savitri mocked at him.

While walking toward Lisa's room, a strange sense of alien happiness took over Loki. He had never experienced something like that ever in his life. The anticipation of new life that was to come filled him with so much joy that he could not think of anything else. His brother was about to become a father. Vishnu and Savitri were about to become grandparents. But more than anything, it was the concept of an "Uncle Loki" that filled his head and heart with untold joy and excitement.

If there was a singular occasion the family needed Loki the most, it was then. In that instant, everything else became secondary. Loki was so taken by the smell of new life that he did not want to leave Lisa's side. He asked Savitri if he could sleep in Sam and Lisa's room. Everyone gladly agreed. That night, for the first time in years, Loki's sleep wasn't infested by his perpetual nightmare.

When Loki visited the daycare the next day, he declared that he would not be dropping by for a few days on account of an urgent family occasion.

"I know Sam is important, but you could at least come by for an hour every day." Kiko disliked the idea of Loki's prolonged absence.

"Sure, I'll be in and out all the time. I hope you guys will not mind. Also, feel free to drop by at my place if you guys wish to. We could do the daycare bit at my place anytime." Loki sounded optimistic.

"That's a great idea. But where's all this fresh energy coming from?" Luke gave words to everyone's thoughts.

"You will know when you will know." Loki had picked that trick from Savitri. "Later." Loki leaped out of the spot, his tail going haywire in wild abandon.

That evening Sam had to return to his job. He gifted Loki a new metal tag called "Uncle Loki" and winked at him like old times. Loki hugged him as he meant it. Sam had given him a gift that was literally above and beyond a metal name tag.

"Take care of Lisa for me. Ask mom to call me." Sam waved Loki goodbye and vanished into the airport crowd.

"Take care of Lisa for me." The words kept reverberating in Loki's heart and mind like some ancient chant of the universe. From that moment on, Loki appointed himself the de facto guardian of Lisa and her unborn baby. Anyone that came to meet Lisa had to get mandatory clearance from Loki. Lisa held her end of the bargain. She wouldn't speak to a man, woman, child, cat, dog, or mouse outside the family unless Loki vetted them first.

When Lisa sat down for breakfast, Loki sat down with her. When she went out for a walk, Loki walked in circles around her. He had a list of everything Lisa needed. He had her water ready even before she felt thirsty. He went on to upgrade to a pair of saddlebags on either side of his back. That had just about everything on the list.

Even when Sam visited Lisa for a day, Loki would be very mindful of Sam not touching her belly, not even playfully. Sam's mischief of trying to touch Lisa's belly would frequently alternate with Loki's mind flashing back to the imaginary thoughts of his mom during her days of pregnancy. He knew pregnant dogs would never get the same care and treatment as pregnant women. The dog-fathers wouldn't even hang around. Ironically, Sam couldn't hang around for long either. But he knew Lisa was in safe company.

A thick week tick-tocked like a shallow minute. Then the big hour came. Lisa had felt some discomfort, and they took her to the hospital. Another couple of days zoomed by, and Loki stayed glued to his spot in the hospital's lobby. He was heartbroken. The doctor wouldn't allow him inside the procedure room. Every time a human would come out of Lisa's room, Loki would ask them about Lisa.

Loki crouched down again, patiently wondering who the baby would resemble. A warm beam of sunlight fell on the lobby floor. Loki laid down, placing his snout right where the sunlight was. He closed his eyes briefly. That week he had done more moving than any other; his body was tired, his limbs had become weak. The sunlight on his nose worked like a balm for his entire body, summarily buzzing him off to sleep.

When Loki woke up, Sam was sitting right beside him. Loki's head was placed between his lap and palms.

"Hey!" Loki said, mildly shaken with Sam's presence.

"Hey," said Sam.

"When did you come?" Loki asked.

"A couple of hours back." Sam smiled.

"What time is it? How long have I been sleeping for?" Loki got up and shook himself.

"It's three in the afternoon, and you've been sleeping for two hours now." Sam laughed a bit.

"Oh my! Where is Lisa?" Loki stood ramrod straight and wiggled himself vigorously.

"She's resting. You took good care of her. I am so proud of you." Sam made Loki sit right back.

"Resting, what do you mean? She was supposed to—" Loki was shocked with disbelief.

"They went to the other room with your nephew. Congratulations! You are an uncle now." Sam had an unmistakable twinkle in his eye.

"My nephew, the nephew. Where is he? Why did you not wake me up?" Loki was furious.

"I wanted to, but Mom said you hadn't slept even for ten hours in the last week. And you were snoring so loud, they almost rang the emergency alarm." Sam broke out into impromptu laughter.

Loki just realized what had happened. A father did not lay beside his newborn child so that he could watch his dog-sibling could find some more sleep. As Sam was laughing, Loki joined him, in parts just relieved of the fact that the baby was born safely and in more significant parts because his brother still loved him the way he used to. Loki gently speared Sam with his furry head. Sam fell on the floor, laughing, and Loki rolled over the floor in joy. Just like that, in the middle of the scantily sunlit hospital lobby, an adult human and an adult dog were going on the floor in the highest spirit of fraternity.

"Congratulations, Sam!" Loki panted as they were still rolling. Even the hospital staff just let them be. Loki knew he couldn't barge into the procedure room. So he thought of the next best thing.

"Now drive me home, Sam. I have to tell my friends and everyone in the neighborhood about it," Loki demanded.

Loki and Sam drove for twenty minutes from the hospital to home. Those twenty minutes, neither of them spoke to the other. Sam just kept looking at the road ahead. Loki leaned out of the window and felt the wind on his cheeks. The wind hadn't felt that good in a long, long while.

The next day, by the time Lisa was home with the baby, half the neighborhood was already back. There was no way he could jostle through so many humans and get into the baby's room. So Loki did the next best thing again. He found Savitri and gave her a long tight hug.

"Thank you, thank you, Mom." Loki held her tighter.

"What for?" she asked Loki.

"For everything, for the surprise." Loki jumped all over the place.

"Okay, okay, now find some rest. Did you see the baby's eyes?" Savitri said as she handed over trays of drinks to the guests.

"No, not yet. There are so many people in there, and half of them are scared of me," Loki complained, grimness playing subtly on his face.

"Fine, I'll tell them it's sleep time for the baby. You tag along," Savitri beckoned Loki.

"Here we go. Introducing baby Vinayak. Tell me, Loki, doesn't he borrow that nose from his mother?" Savitri and Lisa blushed together as they looked at the baby.

Loki did not answer. He just looked and kept looking. He did not blink. He couldn't hear what Savitri was saying. For one brief moment, he paused to look at Lisa. She looked fine. Then he looked at Vinayak again. Those eyes—he had seen those eyes before. Big. Jet-Black. Full of vigor. He was sparkling with life. Those eyes spoke of everything beautiful in this universe. For the second time in one lifetime, Loki lost himself inside those eyes all over again.

"Can you hear me, Loki?" Savitri screamed while hushing her tone.

"Yes, yes, Mom. Sorry, I got lost for a moment. Were you saying something?" Loki recollected himself.

"It's okay, Loks. Even I lost myself in those eyes—all over again." Savitri wiped a tear off her cheek.

"Can I touch him?" Loki asked Savitri.

"Of course, you can," Savitri said.

Loki went near Vinayak, pacing each step with caution. He sniffed all over him from feet to head. Vinayak smelled like life itself—fresh and free from the mundane humdrum of existence. At that moment, as he was lying beside Lisa, the baby seemed like the most carefree soul on the planet.

Like spring summons fresh blossoms, Vinayak had summoned the child in Loki. Bubblier than a moth drawn to the flame, Loki couldn't resist his impulse of licking all over Vinayak's moonlike face. He hopped up the bed, pulled his mouth closer to Vinayak's face, shut his eyes, and started licking. Wait, that didn't feel like Vinayak's face. Loki knew that feeling. Lisa's hand! She'd covered the baby's face with her hand. Why would she do that? Loki sat up aghast. He tried getting to Vinayak's face again. Lisa couldn't help breaking into a laugh. She held his paw, tickled him near the ribs, held him by his core with both her hands and rolled him to the other side of the bed.

"Look at him, Mom," she said hysterically. "He looks like a child whose candy you've snatched." Lisa laughed so hard she had to hold her belly.

"Easy, my girl, don't strain your stomach," Savitri cautioned her.

Shortly after, Loki saw the daylight. Lisa hadn't just covered Vinayak's face with her palm. She'd placed her hand a good couple of inches away from his face. She might even have distanced it farther away as Loki started licking on it. She did not want his tongue anywhere near her child.

Loki lay there beside Lisa, somewhat irritated, if not totally miffed. After a while, he got down from the bed to watch Vinayak sleep. That wasn't the first time Lisa had tickled Loki playfully. She'd been doing that since the first day she met him. But then it felt different. It felt more precautionary than playful, more preventive than protective. A strange silence followed. With every moment of silence, Loki felt a somewhat more profound sense of insult. Savitri was quick to take stock as she egged him on to grab some supplies from the store.

Later that evening, the F5 had a blast at Loki's place. They couldn't believe how happy Loki was, given that he was all sullen with grief barely a week back.

"Am I the only one that can't believe what I am just seeing?" Pixie said, waving for more lemonade.

"Gosh! This lemonade is straight out of heaven. You should get a barrel of this stuff every day to the daycare." Kiko gulped down another glassful.

"Wait, what can't you believe, Pixie?" Luke asked.

"This guy, Loki. He's unbelievable," Pixie gushed.

"Why do you say that?" Weekday was intrigued.

"Why do I say that? I mean, just look at him. Barely a week back, he seemed to have lost all interest in life itself," Pixie answered. "And look at him now! He looks like a new father himself." She looked into Weekday, who was already three lemonades down.

"Oh that! You will know when one of your girls has a child. You might even feel like the de facto mother." Weekday knew things others didn't.

"My child or not, Vinayak is my heart," Loki declared with immediate enthusiasm.

"Easy there, Loks. Humans have broken a million dog hearts. Dogs have retaliated with precisely zero." Kiko could not stop herself from issuing a Loki a soft warning, almost stopping Luke from saying anything by placing her paw on top of his.

The essence of Kiko's warning stayed with Loki. Only that morning, something vital was conveyed to him ever so subtly.

"Been there, Kiko. I have thought this through. But do you remember what Weekday told us about what Steve Martin said?" Loki held this head high.

"Be so good they can't ignore you," Weekday muttered those words like he was reminiscing a line from the book of his own life.

"Yes. And Nelson Mandela said something about our choices reflects our hopes and not our fears," Loki summoned more historical support.

"You win, Loks. I can beat you in an argumentative fight in the middle of my sleep but not when you are invoking history at this rate. Some more lemonade this way, please," Kiko reluctantly conceded defeat.

Kiko might have lost that argument. But she knew Loki was aboard a speeding train that was entering a tunnel cut through a mountain, only the tunnel was there just inside Loki's mind. The mountain itself was as opaque as mountains can be. She also knew that no matter how hard the

F5 tried, they couldn't get the tunnel out of his head. How can you possibly wake up someone that's just pretending to sleep?

And deep inside his own heart, Loki knew too, even if it was a speck of black in a sea of gold. But his imagination was galloping in circles like a mare chasing her most flowery dream. At the center of the ring was the smiling baby Vinayak with his jet-black eyes.

"I don't think I'll be so frequent at the daycare in the coming weeks. Could you guys do me a favor and drop by once in a while?" Loki gathered his focus and tried to regroup his thoughts.

"Hey! You don't even ask. We are all here. Anytime you need us, just send out a word." Luke placed his paw on Loki's shoulder.

Over the next few months, Loki visited the daycare just once on Pixie's birthday. His days, and sometimes even nights, had revolved around baby Vinayak, who he lovingly called Baby V. He'd get Lisa every little thing she needed for Vinayak. In the day, Loki took extraordinary care to push Vinayak's small cradle around the house with just the right force. He'd even guide Lakshmi around as she'd pick a new toy every other day for Vinayak.

When Vinayak went to sleep, Loki watched him sleep like a little child watching the moon for the first time. He would keep gazing at the baby until the point he would fall asleep. As Vinayak grew a little bigger, Lisa and Loki would tour him all around the house and sometimes around the backyard too. Loki even introduced Vinayak to his little bird friend Michael.

The buzzing bonhomie between Loki and Vinayak wasn't free from limitations though. The frequency of Loki's toenails-cutting ritual had gone up from once every fifteen days to once every three days.

"Why do I have to cut my toenails so often?" Loki once asked Savitri for the third time in a week. He had gotten considerably uneasy from the frequent nail cutting.

"I told you already, Loki. You could hurt Vinayak accidentally." Savitri wasn't enjoying that recurring conversation either. And it wasn't hurtful for Loki alone. She would be equally uncomfortable.

In so many ways, Loki was closer to Savitri than her children. And yet she couldn't let him love Vinayak the way he'd naturally do. It split her heart every time Lisa would subtly shove him away whenever he got too close to Vinayak.

The little misery compounded as Vinayak grew older and started crawling around the house. The first to take the hit was Loki's toy basket. That was a world in itself, the toy basket. It had all kinds of fluffy stuff: balls, monkeys, snakes, Frisbees, fidget spinners, air pumps, air horns, bungee cables—basically just about anything you'd need to go backpacking in the woods.

A younger Loki would play all around the house with all the funky stuff in the basket. His favorite by some distance was the monkey with the long tail. When the fluffy monkey first came, he was the same size as Loki. Little Loki would clinch its tail in his mouth and circle the house from one end to the other. Like all small children, he'd innocently claim the monkey and him were inseparable, that he was Loki's best friend.

Loki grew bigger and bigger with time. But the monkey sat there just the way he was— small, dainty, and waiting to be loved. With time, Loki wouldn't play with him as much. But whenever he'd feel low, he'd sit by the monkey's side and bury his nose under his tail. That would remind him of simpler times when Loki was the only prince in the castle.

Then one morning Loki's monkey vanished. And with it, the full basket of toys. Loki looked everywhere—living room, Sam's room, Lakshmi's room, Vishnu and Savitri's room, Vinayak's play area, the backyard, every inch of floor in the property. Was the monkey fooling around? Did the monkey climb up a tree?

"Mom, do you know where my toys are?" Loki asked Savitri.

"Oh them. Those toys are up on the shelf," Savitri remarked with a smile.

"Why are they up on the shelf? Like, I am used to having them by the hall, near the fireplace. Can we please have them back where they belonged?" Loki said with superficial animosity.

"You know Vinayak, right? Ever since he's started crawling, everything he can get his hands to ends up inside his mouth," Savitri said with the same animation.

"Oh! Right, that thought didn't cross my mind. You are right. I just got worked up about not seeing the little monkey I used to play with." Loki breathed a sigh of relief.

"Yes, the monkey. I remember that one. You used to play with it all the time when you were a little boy," Savitri recalled.

"How I used to love that little one!" Loki laughed at himself.

"Haha! Did you? I always thought you two were at war. Vinayak took after you and started chewing his tail. So we had to dispose of the monkey." Savitri smiled regretfully.

"Dispose? What do you mean 'dispose'?" Loki was alarmed by the level of openness in Savitri's words. She, of all people, knew how important the monkey was to Loki.

"It could have been dangerous for the baby, Loks. You know how sensitive babies are." Savitri was expecting more maturity from Loki.

"Yes, yes. I did not think of it that way. I should have. Maybe I acted impulsively. Maybe I am just used to seeing the monkey around the house." Loki pretended to be the mature guy he was not.

"I am sorry, Loks, I didn't quite realize the toy still meant something to you," Savitri said apologetically.

"You're good, Mom. Please don't say sorry, it was just a toy after all." Loki hated Savitri apologizing way more than he ever loved the monkey.

Loki never saw that monkey again. Just like his childhood, it vanished in the whirlwind of a time. He did feel bad about losing it for a while. But he understood the difference between being a child and taking care of one. He knew Vinayak's safety mattered way more than a soft toy and its fluffy tail. Like any other mature guy, he let the monkey pass.

Between burying the child in his heart to heartfully owning the child in the home, what Loki particularly enjoyed was reminding Lisa of Vinayak's regular appointments with the doctor. Part of that was because those were the only two times in the week Loki spent substantial time outside of the house. Like Loki, Savitri and Vishnu had also dedicated a significant part of their lives to Baby V. However, Vishnu did not stop taking Loki out for his walks in the morning. It was just that they were so brisk and short that they almost ended before they began.

But Loki could not care less about shorter walks in the morning. All he wanted to do was to keep the promise he had made to his brother—Loki had promised Sam he'd stay near Vinayak and Lisa all the time. What enthralled Loki was how Vinayak was reciprocating his love. One of the first words that the baby said was "Lolo." The family instantly knew what it meant. Loki loved Vinayak. And Vinayak loved him back.

Vinayak oozed truckloads of cuteness. And for the first time in his life, Loki felt truly responsible for someone. He felt like an adult dog. Moreover, despite his closeness with Vinayak, he always remembered what Savitri had told him when he saw Vinayak for the first time—no tongue, no teeth, and no claws. That had turned out to be the most challenging part for Loki. He would want to lick all over Vinayak's face and maybe even part his little hair with his tongue.

He knew he could not do that. He knew Lisa wouldn't let him do that. No one had told that to him about the new mother. But you don't always hear the truth. Sometimes you just feel it. His mother would never have let someone else lay a hand on him when he used to be a baby. Yet Loki was constantly battling himself in holding back from loving Vinayak the way he wanted to love. A strange and vague sense of discrimination had crept in him, keeping from getting too close to Vinayak. There was still residual hesitation in him even if there was a fair chance it had evaporated from the rest of the family.

Nevertheless, all that mattered to Loki was the permanence of the smile on Vinayak's little face. If you'd have asked Loki then, he'd happily walk on broken glass if that added a little tickle to Vinayak's giggle.

But what in life could be genuinely permanent? The train was ever so close to the mountain. And Loki was inches away from discovering the reality of the tunnel.

One afternoon, for some odd reason, Loki was feeling abnormally sleepy and Vinayak, doubly so. Savitri had paused briefly at the neighborhood store while returning from the clinic. Something in the backyard made a sharp, crackling noise. Loki was instantly upon his feet, hastily shaking off his sleep. Lisa got up too.

"Check on Vinayak, I'll be back from the backyard," Loki said to Lisa with a look of caution on his face.

"Okay," Lisa said with a twitch on her lips.

"It's all right, Lisa. Close the door behind me. Don't wake up Sam. He's just gone to sleep." Loki stepped out into the backyard.

Hola! It was Michael, the birdling that Loki had saved in the backyard a while back. He and Loki had become good friends since Loki had saved his life. But that afternoon, Michal seemed a little strange to Loki. He did not look in great shape. Why was he there so late in the afternoon? And Loki could still not locate the source of that shrill sound.

"Hey, Michael! Is everything all right?" Loki asked from a distance. Michael said nothing, just gave a confused nod. "What up, Mike? So late in the afternoon! I was expecting to see you in the morning." Loki went nearer to Michael, mildly confused at his disposition. Lisa slowly opened the door and peeked out to see what was going on.

Michael still could not accord a proper reply. He walked a couple of shaky steps toward Loki and fell flat on his face inside the tall grass, effectively becoming invisible. Loki rushed to find out what was wrong. Lisa stood at the entrance, nervously watching along.

"Hey, panther," a voice said from inside the grass.

"Who's that?" Loki paused in shock right before he reached Michael and looked around him.

"Vinni, they call me Vinni." A nosy raccoon popped out of the grass a few feet from Michael. Loki looked at Michael, who looked helpless.

"This is Nikki, and he is Tony." Vinny pointed toward two more raccoons that popped out of the grass from two other directions.

"What are you guys doing here?" Loki ground his teeth.

"We are here to exact revenge," said the fourth raccoon from behind, effectively forming a square with Loki, a writhing Michael at the center of it.

"What revenge? There's a baby in the house. You guys have to leave now," Loki said grimly.

"Allen of the House Coon. Does that name ring a bell?" asked a fifth raccoon rising out of the grass.

Then a sixth raccoon sprang out and repeated, "Avenge Allen of the House Coon."

Loki stood there vacant, nearly out of his wits. What was even happening around him? There was more drama than he could handle at that point. As if that wasn't enough already, something even more unprecedented happened. Before Loki could think another thought, about two dozen more raccoons emerged from nowhere, almost filling every square inch of the backyard.

"Avenge Allen of the House of Coon!" thirty-odd raccoons screamed in unison.

Dazzled by what he saw, all Loki could do was pull Michael close to himself. For a moment, Loki was scared to the hilt. He'd never seen aggression in such large numbers. Then he recollected himself. He quickly walked in a circle around Michael and clenched his paws tightly.

"No, I do not know any Allen or Coon. I repeat, you guys need to leave. There's a human baby in the house." Loki circled backward as he spoke, preparing himself to handle aggression from any direction.

"Oh, Allen, you know too well," said Nikki.

"Avenge Allen of the House of Coon," every other raccoon sang in the chorus.

"You killed him at this very spot." Vinni engaged from a distance.

"Oh! So it's about him." Loki was shocked at the suddenness of his realization.

"Let it be understood that he was fairly and adequately warned." Loki immediately realized he was in the middle of inalienable trouble.

"And is that why you did not turn up in the morning, Mike?" Loki threw a distraught look at Michael.

"Avenge Allen of the House of Coon. Hu hu hu," the raccoons repeated a fourth time.

"They had me by the throat. I am sorry, Loki," Michael said meekly. Michael had let down Loki. But even in the middle of the commotion, Loki realized the poor bird had little say. He knew he had to protect Michael. That was if he could defend himself.

"Don't be sorry anymore. We will release you of your pain. Avenge Allen . . .," one quirky raccoon said as she flung herself toward Michael. Loki moved quickly on his feet, turned toward her in a flash, and deflected the raccoon's blow, burying her paw inside the grass.

"Please. Don't do this. I do not want any more blood. Leave us be, and we will walk our ways." Loki softened his tone.

"We will not leave this place. You shall fall at the same spot our brother had fallen," Vinny declared war.

"Dusk or dawn, we fight till you fall!" Tony went ballistic.

"We fight till you fall!" everyone else followed.

Loki knew he barely stood a chance against thirty-odd raccoons. Not many dogs did. He was staring at a certain death, both for himself and for Michael. He had to act quickly and decisively if either of them wanted to see the sunset that evening. So he moved around his spot slowly, hoping to find a potential exit somewhere.

"Lisa!" Loki shouted at the top of his voice.

While Loki was in the middle of a hot spat with the raccoons, he did not notice when Lisa had passed out right where she was standing. She was lying with her eyes closed, her back to the wall and her head falling over to one side. Loki's heart melted. His vision became diluted as his tear glands loaded a couple of eyefuls. And in the haziness of his being, he saw little Vinayak slowly crawl out of the door Lisa had left open. He thought his heart would pop out of his mouth. He physically felt that.

Just then, a couple of sharp claws landed on his back as one of the raccoons flung a paired kick at him. The skin on Loki's back tore, he fell on the ground. A narrow stream of blood gushed. All the haziness that had built up in Loki instantly fumed out.

"No. No, no, no. You cannot do this. The baby is out. Have me. Kill me if you want. But outside, not here. Let me take the baby and his mother inside. I beg of you." Loki almost sounded disoriented.

"Ah! That's it then. There's a child around. We can leave peacefully for now," a well-meaning raccoon said.

"Right, I promise I won't fight you if you let the child and his mother be." Loki sighed.

"Just one condition," the cunning Nikki said.

"What condition?" Loki looked her in the eye.

"We shall have the baby—one of yours for one of ours. We'll then see how happy you drive that BMW of yours," Nikki codified an unthinkable punishment for Loki.

"Not as long as I am breathing." Loki exhaled like a venom-spitting cobra, his jaws trembling with anguish for the raccoon's audacity.

"There's a time when you stand your ground and fight like a hero. Then there's a time when you run for your life like the puny you are. The problem with you, Mr. Panther, is you do not know when to do what. You feel like too much of a hero to have any real courage in life." Nikki was as vicious as she was cunning.

"Can any of you do some real fighting, or all you can do is just talk?" Loki had had enough. He was clearly out of patience with the little furballs.

"You shall know about that in a short while from now," Tony said, licking his claws like an eagle, only there wasn't an eagle on the continent that looked half as funny as him.

"Avenge Allen of the House of Coon!" Nikki yelled.

"Avenge Allen of the House of Coon," the band followed.

"Let's start with the man-cub first. That will light up the dog's tail all right," Tony said as he looked at Vinayak and signaled a charge at him to the other raccoons.

"That's the last time I will hear that in this lifetime!" Loki rendered at the top of his pitch. He blocked another punch from a raccoon and landed a sharp jab on the chest of another. The others rallied up in advance of an attack in which he was heavily outnumbered.

"Bring it on, you little snitches." Loki ground his teeth as he grabbed a raccoon by the collar and flung it over the fence halfway through a neat 180-degree turn. He flapped his ears to clear the auditory inertia and marked his ground like a hound in full readiness of battle.

The flying raccoon landed on the concrete floor outside the backyard, reeling and screaming in pain. Another couple quickly deserted the verdure and ran to the rescue of the injured. Loki slapped the living hope out of one that was trying to edge near Vinayak. He kicked another one in the groins. That one deserted the backyard and sang promises never to return.

"Try that stunt again, and I'll make it the very last stunt of your life." Loki smeared with zeal as he shook off some blood, barely realizing his skin on the back had punctured.

"And this one? Does he matter, or will we consider him the pawn on the board?" That was Vinny. He had clutched Michael's throat.

"Arghh!" Loki groaned within himself, feeling the pain of the wound on his back for the first time.

He knew it was time to make a tough decision. And he had no more than a split second to make that decision. Michael was already heavily injured. He had been Loki's friend ever since the day the latter rescued his life. The two raccoons that had gone out to save the wounded came back with bad news for the House of Coon. Vinny was so furious. He was about to break Michael's neck right then.

"Don't do it!" Loki shouted. "I'll not hurt anyone else if you let him go." He thought that would buy him some time.

In the middle of some intensely heavy panting and baloney of blood-thirsty raccoons, Loki had to bargain between two impossible options: the life of Vinayak or the presence of Michael. If he'd let Michael die, what was the point of saving him in the first place? And what was the end of friendship when he could not defend a friend who was incapable of defending himself? And Vinayak? How could any power on the planet lay a finger on Vinayak while Loki was still breathing? How could Loki live for another day if anything happened to Vinayak?

"Don't worry about me, Loki. Save your family. I am sorry I brought trouble to your door." Michael's voice broke down just like his body.

"Ah! So one of the heroes is sacrificing? How endearing! I am so stoked." Vinny seemed like one of those cruel villains that like to break the weak and innocent before ending them. He just had that look about his left eye. He must have been blind in the right eye because it had a leaf patch, which itself was surprisingly green for a creature so black of heart. But that left eye of his was cruelty personified. It had grown a distinct liking to deriving enjoyment out of others' suffering, especially if he was the cause of it.

As Vinny tightened his grip on Michael, Nikki moved toward Vinayak. Luckily, Loki found a pebble near him. He clutched the stone with his back leg and leaped toward Nikki. A stray raccoon jumped behind him.

Like he was a character from a computer game played by an overzealous child, Loki nutmegged the rock through the flying raccoon's legs and onto Vinni's temple. Vinni groaned with pain, and Michael wriggled out of his dirty claws. Then Loki flung his body vertically down, surprising the raccoon behind him twice in as many seconds. The flying raccoon crashed straight into Nikki, and the two toppled over each other like bowling pins. Loki dealt them discounted blows— six apiece.

"You all right, Baby V?" Loki quickly checked on Vinayak.

As Vinny grunted in pain, he didn't realize when the little bird had slipped out of his clutch. Michael knew what he had to do. With all that he had left in him, Michael flapped his little wings and took off the ground. Then Michael swiveled up and around Vinny as the raccoon made a ridiculous attempt at trampling Michael under his feet.

Michael rose higher and flew farther from Vinny, dodging successive blows from another couple of raccoons. Loki pinned one down by the throat and watched Michael, sharing the amazement of the other raccoons. Even Vinayak couldn't take his eyes off the action, gleefully gazing at the display in front of him.

"Fly, Michael, fly. Save your life. I will handle these nincompoops!" Loki shouted, still trying to catch his breath.

But Michael of House Finch had other plans. Like a fray sheet of ash shooting off the flame, he swiftly rose and circled across Vinny. After he had gathered sufficient altitude, he folded his wings pithily backward, gathering weight near his tail and extended his sharp beak, piercing the wind immediately ahead of him. Michael looked down and aimed. Then like an eagle blessed by the spirit of a dove, he descended upon Vinny.

Meanwhile, Loki cracked an extra couple of skulls at the House of

Coons. Vinny could hardly tell the grass from his elbow. Michael was about to strike the back of his head like an arrow from heaven.

"Watch your back, Vinny," Nikki flipped out, warning Vinny.

Alas! The warning came a little too late. By the time the raccoon turned, his sky was filled with the magnifying beak of the finch he was clutching by the throat seconds back. Michael's beak tore through Vinny's left eye like a vindictive spear tearing through green timber. A splash of blood erupted from Vinny's last eye, and the raccoon descended, crashing down into the green. Bewildered, Vinayak clapped his hands frantically on his little thighs.

"My eye, my eye, my—" Vinny lost his mettle. His lips still moved, but he couldn't let out another word.

"Woohoo, that's my boy!" An exhilarated Loki leaped to guard Michael against the others, partly out of the zeal to congratulate his teammate on scoring an impossible homerun. The raccoons were stunned with what they saw. More than their eyes, it was their spirits that had taken a hit.

"You will pay for it," a muscular raccoon lunged at Michael. Loki rapped him by his neck, kicking the hell out of his arrogant, oversized behind.

"At least your friends will remember you went down fighting a hero, ignorant idiot!" Loki screamed at the reeling Nikki.

"Enough!" yelled an elderly lady at the House of Coon, her pitch so shrill; she out-shouted the cumulative chaos across the yard. "Retreat, I tell you all. We shall live to see another day. Remember the House of Coons. We shall have our vengeance," she said.

The raccoon lady stopped all the remaining three and a half raccoons from advancing any further. Most of the healthy raccoons had already fled the yard. Some were lying unconscious, and others heavily injured. She had made the smart call, she knew Loki wasn't worried about his life, and that made him bounteously dangerous. If the raccoons didn't stop there, the sun would've set on the House of Coons that afternoon. Thankfully enough, the timely call to peace shook Loki out of his blood frenzy too.

"Leave now, and there will be no more blood today, I promise you that," Loki resonated the old lady's wisdom, releasing a raccoon that he had clutched.

"You win this battle. Let us take our fallen heroes so we can honor them," the old raccoon hung her head down before Loki. The sob in her voice was unmistakable. She was in deep pain and anguish. She wanted to lose no more from her family. That immediately softened Loki.

"I am sorry I had no other . . ." Loki was about to offer a few consolatory words to the raccoon when the most unexpected thing happened.

"Loki! What the hell do you think you are doing?" It was Savitri. She was back from the store. Like every other average person would have been, she was astonished at what was in front of her.

"Mom, I can . . ." Loki was startled by Savitri's shouting. She had yelled at him in the past. But he had never heard that voice of hers. It was like a baby girl had seen a monster under the bed.

"No, do not speak. You do not speak one more word!" Savitri accessed an even louder pitch, rattling Loki numb. She picked up a clueless Vinayak in her lap and shook Lisa. She feared the worst at first. But fortunately, Lisa responded and asked for water.

Loki sunk into the grass, his mind blanked with all that had transpired in the last few minutes. He couldn't believe what Savitri had done to him within the space of a few words. He couldn't think Savitri believed he had willingly endangered her family, that she felt that he was different from her family. The little girl hadn't seen a new monster. She had discovered one living inside her own house. Within a split second, Loki and Savitri went from being an inseparable mother-child duo to two people who had broken each other's hearts with such apparent cruelty. It was inexplicable at so many levels.

"My child, my little child." Savitri kissed Vinayak, frantically checking all over him for wounds. She held Lisa by her waist and took the two of them inside. Loki was sitting there on the grass, out of breath, and by all means, out of his mind.

Loki lay there like someone who had lost all hope in life. The grass around him was red with blood, some his own and some of the ones he had slain. Michael was there somewhere. Loki could feel him breathing, but he didn't know if the bird would make it. Loki lay still there, not even a thought to keep him company. He was hurt physically, but more than hurt, he was broken. He was so broken, he did not know where he should've gone, whether he should've even moved from his place. At that moment, he did not want to live anymore. He just wished his wounds were deep enough. Loki closed his eyes for a moment. It was slowly getting dark.

*   *   *

At that moment, everything had come to a standstill. What Loki was experiencing was more than just hurt; it was a deep sense of loss, loss of an irreversible variety. He felt his mind expand and fill the entire backyard. A strange, almost alien sense of calm descended upon him. Loki felt like he'd lost everything, he had lost the bliss of ignorance, and he'd lost the fear of losing. He'd lost the guilt of maiming a clan of fellow earthlings who were just in their right to avenge one of their own.

Loki was so deep inside the ocean of despair that he never knew if he'd ever see the sun again. When they'd taken away V from the puppy store, he'd just scratched the surface of the ocean. He had felt pain and helplessness. He had experienced anguish and hopelessness. He'd been through despair and a while later, even detachment. More than anything else, he felt lonely. Never after the day V had left did he ever feel so alone, so unimaginably remote.

So long back, when he'd lost the company of V, he did not even fully understand what loneliness meant. His senses weren't as developed; his experiences not as vivid. But that time, it was like he was lying down on a surgery table. The surgeon was cutting through his flesh. He could hear the metal tear his skin and muscle and feel every inch of the pain, all while pretending the anesthetic had worked. It hadn't.

Loki was in a state of consciousness that wouldn't typically be considered sleep. He could hear Michael breathe. He could vape the flies buzz around. Loki could feel the wind on him and smell the stench of blood it carried. He could sense Lisa and Vinayak were unharmed. He perceived everything that his senses could perceive. Yet Loki did not feel conscious the way a dog feels conscious.

Loki's mind went back to the time he'd spent at the puppy store without V. During his puppy store days, Loki had been indefinitely counting days and nights after V had left. He was living life like a depressed dog as if he did not intend to live anymore. He'd eat when offered food, drink when he'd find water, and keep his eyes shut to all forms of play and entertainment.

Like ocean waves disappearing into the ancient horizon, thoughts of V slowly subsided from Loki's mind. For a few moments, his mind was blank with a painful vacancy. Then like the flickering flame of a candle in the center of a dead galaxy, Sam's face floated up at the center of Loki's rapidly expanding mind. When everything else had seemed bleak, a sure lively teenager who incidentally owned the most possessed pair of jet-black eyes had chanced upon him. That teenager had given Loki a second chance at life, and he'd given Loki a home. Loki wouldn't have the experience he had if Sam did not find him.

The calm in Loki made way for yearning. His heart yearned for Sam. Sam saw him when everybody else was blind. Sam understood him when no one else did. He was always there for Loki, both before and after the family accepted him.

"Sam would understand," Loki said to himself.

Or would Sam? It was Sam's child that was endangered by Loki. That was at least what the situation implied.

*   *   *

"Loki, Loki!" Sam shouted in his sleep. He must have seen a horrible dream.

Sam had been sleeping all through the backyard battle. He sprung out of his bed and immediately sensed the pandemonium downstairs. When Sam reached the ground floor, he saw Savitri and Vishnu sprinting from one room to the other. Lisa was on the bed, singing Vinayak a lullaby while rocking him in her arms.

"What happened?" Sam asked Lisa hastily.

"The raccoons, lots of them. Vinayak was . . ." Lisa tried to mellow things down.

"Loki! Where is he? Where's Loki?" Sam cut Lisa in between. He had already realized Vinayak was safe.

"He's outside. He can't seem to get past his hunting bug. Even if that means endangering the family," Savitri said from behind.

"How long?" Sam hushed.

"Ten minutes, maybe fifteen," Lisa said. Sam rushed to the backyard. "Mom, it wasn't Loki's fault though . . .," Sam faintly heard Lisa say those words as he rushed out of the backyard.

Loki's back had stopped bleeding when Sam reached him. Thankfully! But the heart? Who knew? What Sam knew was there was pain on Loki's face, the type of pain that visits you when people who have held dear all your life suddenly turn back and say you are not worth it. Honestly, it's even deeper than that—they declare you unfit to be considered family.

In the middle of his semicomatose lull, Loki felt a usual presence around. He drew in the air sharply a couple of times. He knew who that was. Yet he did not want to open his eyes, fearing Sam would judge him too.

Sam gently placed his hand on Loki's forehead. "Are you hurt, big boy?" Sam asked.

Sam's words were more soothing than the fallen leaves of autumn. Loki knew he could open his eyes. Sam was lying facedown right in front of Loki. His jet-black eyes were watching Loki's. There might even have been a couple of teardrops as well, Loki couldn't tell.

"Sam, I can explain," Loki said, the pain in his voice visible from miles.

"Don't. Don't say a word." Sam hugged Loki's face tightly. He still did not know what exactly had happened. But he knew something else, something more substantial and universal. Loki would never, in his breathing existence, hurt or cause hurt to anyone in the family.

Loki's heart sank again, this time with vindication. His mind rapidly started recovering from the lull. He drooled at Sam's eyes some more.

"How's Vinayak?" Loki asked.

"Perfect! What could happen to him when the big ol' Uncle Loki is around?" Sam playfully jeered at Loki. "Now we are going to the vet or what?" Sam asked.

"Is Mom still mad at me?" Loki looked the other way.

"Are you crazy? Of course not! Now move your heavy bum and get into the car. Drag your little birdie too." Sam got up, shook off the grass from his clothes, and ran inside for his car keys. Savitri came running out, followed by Lakshmi.

"I am so sorry. I did not know . . ." Savitri sat weeping near Loki. She was so guilt-ridden that she did not even have the courage to touch or caress Loki.

Sam started the car. Loki lifted himself off the grass and slowly walked to pick Michael.

"You don't need to say that, Mom. There's no reason to apologize." Loki could not look Savitri in the eye. Lakshmi helped his limping form to the car.

"I wish I could be the mother you deserved." Savitri broke down, crying.

"Pull yourself up, Mom. You are more than I deserved," Loki said Savitri as he pushed Michael and himself into the car. As the car sped, Loki zoned out once again.

While returning from the vet, Loki and Sam dropped Michael at his home in the woods. The bird had looked death in the eye—twice. And both times, it was Loki that saved him. Loki was to Michael what Sam was to Loki—a guardian angel and so much more.

"You feeling all right, champ?" Sam asked cheerfully.

"Yeah, never felt better," Loki said with a smile.

No, Loki had felt better, a lot better in the past. He remembered the time when he first saw Michael. The finches could barely touch his skin through his thick coat, and Savitri had raised hell. She wouldn't let a fly touch him. She would ransack every strand of hair on his body for traces of wounds. Loki did not even want to go to the vet, but Savitri dragged him nonetheless.

Then there was this day. Loki was ready to give his life to save Vinayak. If Vinayak had a scratch on him, it would mean Loki was long dead already. And yet Savitri did not so much as look at Loki when he could barely move in the backyard after risking his own life to save Vinayak's. Loki realized that for every person in that family, himself included, Vinayak's life was dearer than his own, perhaps rightly so, Loki thought to himself.

What was so grand about a dog's life in the first place? Once you are a dog, you stay a dog for life. If fortune smiles, you find a decent home, enough food, and get to wag your tail at a few humans who cast at you the illusion of a family.

Vinayak himself had been such an inexplicable boon in Loki's life. Ever since Loki had seen his moonlike face and liberated himself in its service, the nightmares had vanished. The troublesome thoughts about V had subsided. Vinayak had done to Loki what even the F5 could not.

Maybe it was because, in parts, Loki had lost his individuality and found new meaning in the service of someone he believed was purer than himself. You lose a chunk of your pain when you devote yourself to other people's happiness. In that regard, to some extent, even unknowingly, Loki was selfish in his love for Vinayak. But suffering and pain always find a way to creep back into life.

Individuality struck back that night and with it, the nightmare. One cruel blow of fate had broken the cocoon of happiness that Loki had built around him.

Before Loki went to bed that night, he wanted to check on Vinayak. But he did not want anyone to know about it. He sneaked into Vinayak's room. Vinayak was fast asleep and deeply peaceful, his head buried in his mother's bosom. What else does a baby even need? What else could Loki ever desire?

That night Loki felt particularly restless. His mind had nestled with thoughts about his siblings and his mother. A light shiver flew across his body, subtly making him aware of every inch of skin on him.

Then came by a startling thought: *Does Mom remember me too?* If Loki's mom was alive, did she remember her children? Did she miss them? For Loki, it was a damning insight, one of reciprocation, some distant nostalgia that never existed.

*   *   *

When Loki finally drifted into sleep, he saw a movie the trailer of which had played in his mind over a thousand times. Only this time, for a moment, it went from bad to briefly pleasant. But that hadn't been a pleasant kind of day.

Inside the dream, Loki saw his mom all by herself. She had just given birth to six or seven pups. Her appearance spelled out tiredness and fatigue, but her eyes were full of love and hope. The place seemed like a corner of a large and dusty hall. She wasn't the only new mother in there; there were others too.

The pups were playing behind the mother's back around her tail. Some even on her head. A cute one was amazed to feel two holes inside the big dog's nose. She immediately checked her nose, and it just felt like one big hole. That amounted to cheating. So the little dog drummed her nose against her mother's as punishment to the latter. Scores were settled, at least for that moment.

"You, hey you!" someone nudged the baby Loki.

"Me? Are you talking to me?" Loki couldn't see this guy.

"Yes, you. Can you see me?" the other pup asked.

"No, I cannot. Can you see me?" baby Loki asked.

"No, me neither." The fellow pup seemed just as stumped.

"Oh! No! No, no, no. Don't tell me we are born blind," a third pup joined.

"Our lives are ruined then. We will miss out on all the good stuff there is to see out there." Baby Loki's hopes suffered the first blow of reality.

"Oh! Stop it, little ones. Will you now?" the mother dog said, licking every pup within reach of her tongue.

"And who are you, lady? Are you our mother?" Loki tried to play the fool with the old dog.

"Yes, that. Or I am a ghost from one of your past lives, maybe the one that made you blind." The mother dog was equal to the task.

"Why would you say something like that, Mama? Tell us, please. Why are we blind?" a pup asked.

"None of you are blind, all right. Just a few days, children! You will have eyes on you very soon," the mother reassured her litter.

While this was going on, a couple of Loki's siblings could not care less that they had no eyes. They were just totally blissed out about having found a big tail they could hop over.

"Why are your furs so soft and deep?" Loki asked, burying his head in her furs.

"My furs are soft and deep so your nose stays warm, naughty one. Now help me get a proper tongue on you." Loki's mother licked him with all the love and care in the universe.

Isn't that the most beautiful thing ever—a mother's love for her child embedded by nature through millennia of evolution across land and sea, continents, and species? A deer loves her fawn, like a frog loves its tadpole, like a human loves her baby, like an eagle loves her nest, like a cheetah loves her cub. There was no exception thousands of years back, and there won't be one as long as organic life exists.

"Your tongue is so wet. I am all water," Loki complained.

"And I am all hunger," another pup cried.

"Poor ones, you must be. Crawl up to this side, and suckle on me for sweet milk." The mother was all ready to feed her children for the first time. Her heart was beating against her chest with joy and fondness.

To Loki and his siblings, that was the first invitation to a feast. Weren't the little ones excited? Maybe a little less excited than they were hungry but excited nonetheless. They crawled toward her breasts from all over and dropped like baby ghosts seeping out of a tin can. As the others latched on to whatever they could, Loki had some difficulty finding a proper nipple.

"The pups are moving, come on now," a burly human noise shot out of nowhere, shattering all the cute dog chatter like a big rock blasting against a pane of glass.

"On it, boss," said an absolute monster of a man. He had a shotgun and wore a snake tattoo on his left wrist right below the thumb. He came steaming toward the pups and snatched them away from the mother one by one. Loki was the first to be lifted and placed inside a big crate. Loki had no idea what was going on or why he had no milk on his lips. Most pups were easy to pluck, some others resisted a bit. But none of them could fight back a seemingly supernatural force.

"No, no! Don't take my pups from me. Let my children have their fill of milk at least," the mother dog wailed in a searing wet voice. She begged the man to return her babies. Her voice started to faint as another thick voice poured into Loki's ears.

*   *   *

"Loki, Loki!" Vishnu called out. "We are late for the walk," he said.

"Mom, Mom! Let me go to my mom!" Loki screamed in the middle of his sleep.

"What happened, Loki?" Vishnu was immediately worried.

"Mom, I saw my mom," Loki blabbered in his sleep, barely able to open his eyes.

"You had a bad dream, big boy? It's okay. Bad dreams lead to good days." Vishnu didn't know what he was encountering.

"No, I saw my mom." Loki woke up, suddenly realizing he was speaking to Vishnu.

Loki got up from his sleep like he'd seen a living ghost. What did he just dream? Could any of that be right? Why did the man with the snake tattoo even exist? Where was Loki's biological father? Why did Vishnu want to go out for a walk? It took Loki a while to ride back to reality and feel the earth beneath his paws.

"Savitri, could you drop by for a moment, please? Our youngest seems to have discovered you in sleep." Vishnu was mildly excited.

"I didn't see her," Loki said grimly.

"Oh, oh, all right." Vishnu realized what he'd just hit.

Savitri came by and joined along. She was still unsure how Loki would react to her presence. She didn't know what she should tell him yet. Which words would have been enough? Savitri had no clue. She had only vaguely understood the kind of emotions she had triggered inside Loki. She just sat there and placed her hand on Loki's neck. Then she slipped her hands below Loki's paws and hoped he'd understand.

Savitri felt like a sinner; there was no way she could make anyone believe how blissfully difficult it was to be a mother. She couldn't. No mother could ever. So she did the only thing she could. She prayed, like all mothers pray. Sometimes all you do is say a silent prayer and hope the universe answers.

Loki knew nothing about how Savitri felt like she knew nothing of his heart. Then it came to him, like a note inside a bottle that had washed ashore sometime back. Loki had the bottle with him for a while now. It was only that night that he happened to open the note. The realization was sacrosanct. Everything else meant nothing. Not Sam, not Vinayak. Not Savitri, Vishnu, or Lakshmi. Loki wanted his *mom*!

"Are we going out to walk or not?" Vishnu reasserted.

"I feel a little heavy in the head, Dad. Can we skip today?" Loki gave Vishnu a confused answer.

"Sure. After all your heroics from yesterday, you deserve some extra rest. Maybe I'll just take a short walk myself." Vishnu overrode the surprise of Loki refusing a walk.

In the living area, Lisa was walking with Vinayak in her lap. The two seemed inseparable. The good thing was no one was planning on separating them. It's a crime against humanity to take such a young child from his mother, only if it is a human mother and a human child. Everybody else is just a pre-evolution sub-creature!

Loki did not want to walk. He did not want to eat. He did not want to speak to anyone. He was breathing somewhere and living somewhere else. Thoughts about his mother flooded his mind awash. All he wanted was to see his mom. He wanted her smell, her fur, the warmth in them, and the rest of the dream. Yet again, he lost himself in his mother's thoughts.

"Dad, can we ride instead?" Loki asked Vishnu moments before he was about to set off.

"Sure, if you want. But where to?" Vishnu was doubly surprised.

"I was wondering if you could drop me off at the daycare. I haven't met my mates in a while," Loki said. The "while" in the statement was a real while since Loki had met his friends at the daycare. It had been a long, long while.

"Hop on then." Vishnu smiled at Loki.

As Loki rode to the daycare, he did not know how his friends would receive his idea, if he could call it that. What he had in mind wasn't just a basic idea; it was a revolution at so many levels. What would Sam and Lakshmi say? Would they approve? Loki was too engrossed with zeal to think of any of it.

"Dad," Loki hushed.

"Yes, tell me," Vishnu answered.

"Do you think Mom loves me?" Loki asked casually.

"More than the world, Loki. I know what happened yesterday was very unfortunate. Maybe she could not tell you, but she kept weeping through the night," Vishnu reassured Loki.

"I know, Dad. She can't sleep when I can't." Loki looked out of the window; a fight was forming within the fight.

"Oh, you children know her better than me, isn't it, Loks?" Vishnu said with a slight grin.

"Maybe, Dad. Can I ask you something, if you don't mind?" Loki posed meekly.

"Definitely, sir. Shoot it." Vishnu could sense the pain in his voice.

"Why can't I go back to my mother?" Loki asked endearingly.

"Who told you that? You can always go back to her. We can turn the car around and go home right now if you want." Vishnu found it challenging to finish his lines without his voice choking up. He could only imagine how deeply everything that had happened must have hurt Loki.

"No, Dad. I am talking about my mom, as in the lady that gave birth to me," Loki answered with a straight face.

Vishnu pulled up the car. He did not believe his ears. What he had just heard was beyond him. His pet dog had been thinking about his family, his own family, the dog group from which he was separated. That was a rattling realization. At some point, Loki must have felt he did not belong to Vishnu's family. Vishnu was as sorry as he was shocked.

"I am sorry, Loki. I am sorry on behalf of everyone else in the family." Vishnu held Loki's palms in his.

"Don't say that, Dad. I want to know. Where is my mom? Why do dogs have to live away from their mothers?" Loki slid his paws out from Vishnu's palms.

"I wish I could tell you, Loki. I wish I knew myself. Just know that there is more truth in life than our little boxes of emotions can handle." Vishnu didn't realize when his eyes had leaked.

Loki did not reply to that. The car started again. As the vehicle moved, hundreds of fallen leaves got further displaced by the wayside.

*   *   *

Vishnu dropped Loki off at the daycare. When he went back home, he did not speak to anyone. He played some music, turned off the lights, and hit the sack, hoping he'd forget that conversation between Loki and him ever happened.

When Loki reached the daycare, the F5 was raving about some new dog movie they'd just watched. Loki heard them from a distance; he did not walk up to them. He was hesitant. He didn't even remember the last time he was at the daycare. Spark and some of his friends were playing around a rope. Loki sat down, silently vaping vibes from all corners.

There seemed to be many new dogs at the daycare. They were excited to see Loki. So like all excited dogs with the bliss of ignorance, they came sniffing at Loki, wagging their little tails in optimism. They might have thought Loki would play with them. But Loki was done with all the play, and he was so done with all the goodness of ignorance.

Over the past months, Loki had barely spent any time at the daycare. So much seemed to have changed at the place he considered his second home. More had changed inside him.

Even the F5 seemed to be at ease without Loki. They missed him rather terribly for a few weeks after Vinayak was born. No conversation seemed funny enough, and no game was as enterprising without their dear friend. For the record, missing someone is a terribly underrated form of intoxication. First, you get used to their absence. Then you grow addicted to it. Like every other addiction, it only gets worse with time. The worst phase is when you want to quit, rather when you are forced. That is when the absence ends, and the awkwardness begins. For Weekday, Pixie, Luke, and Kiko, that moment came with Loki stepping into the daycare.

"Guys, guys," Pixie blurted with a sudden, shrill tone.

"What is it?" Kiko responded.

"There, right there. Do you guys see it?" Pixie pointed out to the open play area.

"Oh my, I can't believe my eyes." Weekday gasped for air.

"Goodness me, what's wrong with him?" Luke was just as puzzled.

"Should we go speak to him?" Pixie pleaded, looking at Weekday with meaningful eyes.

What the F5 saw wasn't the Loki they knew; it was a living, breathing ghost of their friend, of someone lost in a storm within his mind. Something cruel had hit the deepest seat of hope in his heart. If you were a human watching him, you couldn't tell the difference though. He'd seem like any other healthy dog with looks alternating between "cute" and "curious." But it takes a dog to know a dog. The unmistakable brokenness of his countenance, the steely resolve of his spine, and the absolute lack of form on his shoulders—Loki's friends knew he was in the middle of loneliness like he had never known before.

"I said, can we please go speak to him?" Pixie was louder at that time.

Weekday still did not answer; he seemed lost at the mere appearance of Loki. At the peak of their dog days, Weekday and Loki would gnaw into the very clock of each other's routines. They had the kind of friendship where one spoke to the other without talking. They'd eat from each other's plate, hang out with each other's humans, and whatnot! Yet their friendship stood locked in the crosshairs of destiny. Weekday looked at Loki and just kept looking.

"Weekday, can you hear her?" Kiko joined.

"Yes, yes." Weekday's trance was shaken. "Let's go speak to him," he added softly.

Luke and Kiko stood up, walked up to the rope dogs, and told them their play was up. The little dogs showed themselves out, leaving Loki alone at the far end of the green. Like a floating island docking itself to a stagnant, hopeless boat, the F5 walked up to Loki. Kiko, Weekday, Pixie, and Luke sat around Loki like they were standing guard to a precious yet despondent jewel. A thin ray of the morning sun intersected two dogs, and a beam of sunlight fell upon the ground right next to Loki. Loki exhaled sharply and placed his chin between the grass and the sunshine. A moment of solitary tranquility followed.

"Loki," Kiko said and placed her palm softly on Loki's shoulder.

"Hey, I just thought I would lay here by myself for a while," Loki murmured meekly.

"You are not saying you mind us walking across, are you?" Pixie said with a confused smirk.

"No, no. Not at all. Stay, please. I just did not mean to cut you guys between a conversation. So I just thought I'd wait here for a while. Plus, Spark and I were talking about . . ." Loki had thought of that explanation a while back.

"I wouldn't excuse this crime of formality if you didn't look this wasted," Luke said, a suggestive grin playing around the wide end of his lips.

"Now tell us why the longest face in five years or I'll personally tie your tail to a cocktail and spin the Met Gala around it." Pixie zealously tried extracting a smile out of the pile of depression that was Loki.

Loki did not smile. He would be the first to burst out laughing even when Pixie was at her unfunny best. But not then. He just couldn't find that smile. He had lost his smile in the warm depth of his mother's furs the previous night. There was only one way to find it back—one riddled with impossibilities. As such, choosing among possibilities wasn't an option anymore.

Ever since he had made up his mind about finding his mom, Loki wasn't even thinking of possibilities. He had just been formulating, his mind subconsciously mapping a flowchart of his journey to his mom. Deep inside his psyche, he'd metaphorically gone from being an agent to becoming an actor. And such is the universal, all-encompassing nature of commitment. The most stringent commitment dissolves your existence and turns you into something new, perhaps one of many actors in a more significant cause.

Every active thought about his mom turned Loki's body cold with longing. A sudden gush of energy followed, filling his chest, glutes, and limbs with passion; a surge of urgency filled the length of his spine.

"Snake." Loki rose and found a firm hold on the grass with all four paws. He walked out of the four-dog perimeter, brushing past Luke and Kiko.

"What?" Pixie and Weekday said, baffled.

"I need to go." Loki charged. Kiko and Luke leaped in reaction and blocked his way. Pixie and Weekday followed up and reinstated the perimeter.

"You are not going anywhere until we know everything." Weekday meant business.

An air of desperate inquisitiveness filled the hearts of Loki's friends, all his friends, except Luke. Luke was the one with ears to the ground and eyes in the sky. From raptors to raccoons and roosters to robins, Luke had news from everyone that was not friends with humans.

"Is this about yesterday's backyard clash, Loki?" Luke struck a painful but accurate chord.

"You spoke to Michael?" Loki looked up at Luke, meeting someone's eyes for the first time since he arrived at the daycare that day.

"Yes, I did. Someone from the woods brought word that Michael took a rather unusual hit. So I went to check on him in the middle of the night," Luke said, yawning halfway through his lines.

"What exactly are we missing here?" Pixie fumed.

"Loki's family was attacked by the House of Coons. And our boy here politely told them what it means to be an F5 amongst mere earthlings," Luke's heart filled with pride.

Luke was the only other dog in the F5 who had real fighting experience. He had fought for his life before. Every time Luke fought, he maimed another dog, often leaving them with a permanent disability, if not permanent death. Every night that he had fought, he'd thank the creator for letting him live another day and pray for the dog he'd hurt. That fighting was nothing like what they showed in the movies.

But Loki did not just fight for his own life; in fact, he'd considered giving up on his own life so that he could save the life of his family. He never really believed he stood a chance before a full clan of wild animals. But what he did know was his family couldn't meet harm while he was still meeting with life. He won the fight, then he lost!

"And why the depression?" Kiko asked, bemused with Loki's seemingly perpetual passiveness.

"I have decided on something." Loki cut the chase with some somber certitude.

"What have you decided?" Weekday was curiously curious.

"I have decided that . . ." Loki cleared his throat. "I have decided that I need to visit my mother," he said matter-of-factly.

"Wait on! You mean, your real mother, the one from your dreams!" Pixie said in disbelief, her head spinning in all directions of bewilderment.

"Do you even know where she is?" Luke added hastily.

"And what does this visit of yours entails?" Weekday added the most critical quip to the conversation.

Loki shook himself a tad, circled a few paces back and forth, and sat on his spot, giving his head just that much more time to organize his thoughts. His form wasn't shaky anymore, his shoulders were stout, his spine and tail erect with determination.

"I know what you guys are thinking—that the rich dog has lost it, that I have swapped my guardianship whims for filial fantasies. The brittle illusion of a human family had the better of me." Loki distributed the magnitude equally through his words. He drew in a long, loud breath, forecasting heightened potency in the words that were to follow. "I need you guys to know that I hold none of these against you. I hold nothing against anyone. My heart is free of angst and ignorance. Yes, I am driven by desire—the desire to reunite with my mother. But my desire is pure. And purity demands that I be honest with you. I regard each of you dearly." Loki abruptly paused, as if he'd spotted an indefinitely glowing decimal flickering in the distant cloud.

"We are listening." Weekday pressed his foot forward. He was just as fixated at Loki's sameness as everyone else.

"I have, after careful deliberation, decided that I shall leave home." Loki drew in some more air. "I shall leave home and go out to seek my mother. Before you guys ask about it, I do not know where she is, and I do not know how I'll get there. Honestly, I am at sea with how I want to go about this. What I do know is that my search starts now." Loki had never said something as resounding. The ascending resonance of his words filled his mind. Just like the previous day, he physically felt his mind expand.

Loki had said severe things in the past but never something so grimly real. Weekday, Pixie, Luke, and Kiko immediately realized Loki had meant what he'd said about visiting his mother a while earlier. Each of them had the same response to what they'd just heard—a deafening silence. Inside their bundles of silence, each dog riveted in an incoming barrage of thoughts and impulses.

The dogs thought about different things related to Loki, how he'd changed and the sheer malevolence of whatever had changed him. They took a moment to think about their own lives and how the hunch about a similar quest had eluded them. But most importantly, each of them invariably thought about their mothers. The sound of that silence summarily manifested into an outright uproar.

"Your mother is lucky to have a son like you." Pixie wiped off a tear. "I wish my mother was as lucky. Or maybe I am just a coward," Pixie sobbed.

Those words were Pixie's. But both Luke and Kiko were thinking minor variations of precisely those lines. For the first time in their lives, they felt cruelly selfish for not remembering their dog families, for getting lost in the luxuries of a human-centric world. It took them no more than a split second to empathize with Loki.

"I might never know how it feels to come crashing down after investing so much love . . ." Luke tried hard to string together a bunch of stray emotions.

"I am still investing in love. And I will forever invest in love. Loving was never a problem. I was just unaware of the consequences." Loki's voice was steely with resolve. He seemed to have discovered the mystery of that decimal in the sky. A teardrop came and went by. Loki did not attribute even a moment's attention to it.

"Then we shall invest together, and we will seek the love you seek." Weekday looked up. As the only dog in the gang who knew what it meant to feel the mother's furs and then part from them, he knew every bit of that investment was worth it.

"No, no," Loki protested, his heart brimming with gratitude. "I cannot knowingly inflict upon you the path I have so exclusively chosen for myself." Loki tried hard to hide the wetness in his voice.

"I am sure I am speaking for each of us when I say this. If there's anything that tells friendships of a lifetime from situational, need-based companionship, it is the purity of purpose. And the way I see this, there cannot be a purer purpose for all of us." Luke cemented his stand on the issue.

"We have come so far, haven't we?" Pixie fit the space between the four dogs and placed her paw on Loki's. She hugged his leg lightly. Loki lifted the gates off the deluge in his eyes.

"Yes, we have." Kiko hugged Loki.

"We have come so far, and yet we never realized where we were going." Weekday completed Pixie's thought, giving her a lift on his back so she could hug Loki's neck.

"If this is your wish, this is our desire too. That's where we are going." Luke joined the hug.

Loki looked skyward. "I am coming, Mom," he said to a soft, furry cloud.

*   *   *

Teaser to Volume 2 - The adventure has just begun . . .

The F5's real journey has just begun. A long tail of questions still wags.
What road will they take next?
How far will they go?
Will the adventure take a toll on their friendship?
Is Mom still around? Will Loki ever get to meet her?
All in *Adventures of Loki, The Husky 2*, releasing in January 2021.

There was no way Loki could harbor even a shred of scorn about Vinayak in his heart. What did Vinayak even know of the world? The baby had barely seen all the flooring inside his own house. He knew nothing about why the raccoons had come, why Loki fought them, why Savitri yelled at Loki or why Loki was so broken from inside.

The answer to all those questions was the same thing—family. The raccoons had come for their family, they fought for their family, Loki fought them back for his family, Savitri yelled at him for her family, and after the long sunset, Loki yearned for his family—the real family. This whole realization hit Loki the same time that Vinayak's gaze did.

A child's eyes had given him the solace that a thousand words of apology from the adults couldn't. Without losing another second to spite, Loki forgave Savitri and Lisa. The ice spear nestled inside Loki's heart magically vanished. Vinayak's eyes had single-handedly melted a mountain of snow and all the pride with it.

Lightning Source UK Ltd.
Milton Keynes UK
UKHW010817231220
375746UK00008B/259/J